REAL TEX
Secrets to Success

Introduction

Cashes Secrets to Success, the seasoned real state investor.

The reward is yours but first you must labor, plant your thoughts and ideas, harvest them and watch them grow; remember you will sow in tears before you reap with joy. You can put your thoughts and ideas down in black and white or whatever color you prefer. You'll find it fun and challenging and best of all easy. If you are like most the people I know you learn best by having someone show you the way. I won't tell you what to do, I'll show you how to do it and then it's up to you.

One of my favorite sayings is..."If it's to be, it's up to me." When you've decided what you want whether it be wealth, independence or fame, you've made the first and most important step on your journey to success.

What I want to do for you, and I will, if you let me, is stimulating your thought process and motivate your desires together will find the tools along the way. Getting started is the hardest part of any job. If you have the courage to start then with the proper motivation you will have the courage to finish.

Keep away from the people who want to belittle your ambitions, small people do that, but the really great make you feel like you too can be really great.

Most people spend their whole life trading hours for dollars and end up with nothing. Don't end up in the poor house relying on someone else to provide for you. Be the master of your destiny and make a roadmap that will take you all the way. You may have to detour around some rugged roads ahead but be straight and true and you'll find the way to your independence day.

I can read your mind! Right now you're are thinking; "This is all well and good, but where is it taking me?"

Have patience my friend, I'm pouring a solid foundation for the home of your future.

I don't expect anything from you that I'm not willing to give of myself. A good thing to remember is that friends make all your achievements and successes worthwhile. I want to be your friend and when you succeed I want you to remember where the encouragement and motivation came from.

My reward for teaching this material will be your success and your success is one of my goals..

Each day a new door opens to all kinds of experiences and challenges. Meet the day with a smile and say to yourself that nothing no matter how big or how small will pass your attention. Meet all the challenges it brings head on and quench your thirst with its knowledge. Remind yourself that today will be a glorious day.

Frame of mind is a powerful tool and when used with optimism it can make your trip to success so much easier. In my mind there's a picture of the pessimist who sees the difficulty in every opportunity as opposed to the optimist who sees the opportunity in every difficulty. Another good thing to keep in mind is…All things turn out best for the people who make the best out of the way things turn out.

Having wealth and fame is a wonderful achievement, but let me remind you that monetary gain is not always the answer for being a success. Happiness, serenity, and integrity, are just a few of the measurements to success. The ideal solution is to find success in all things.

My one claim to fame is my peace of mind. I've lived a long life and made tons of mistakes. I've tried to make amends for all the harm that I've done but in some cases that's not possible. So instead of making amends I now make repairs. I try to fix the problems of others and that's where I've found my biggest successes.

To help someone who has had their dreams shattered and their lives disrupted is the most rewarding thing in the world. To help someone to find an answer to their dreams and reach their ultimate goals and desires is equally rewarding. I can honestly say that helping others has been my greatest achievement and everything else in life is a bonus. I've had more than my share of bonuses.

This material is aimed at helping you find financial success but I'm greedy and I want you to have it all. As I've explained money and fame is the wrong kind of game if it doesn't include happiness and peace of mind.

If you are ready to find financial security and you want to do it Cashes way. Which I do believe is the easiest way.
Another one of my favorite sayings..."Beginning is Winning." Don't be afraid of making mistakes, the biggest mistake a man can make is to be afraid of making one. I see mistakes as stepping stones to success

Property values have been on a steady climb almost everywhere in the world. They keep rising whether the economy is good or bad. As an investor you'll soon find out just how profitable real estate can be and that it takes little or none of your own money to make money. It's like making money out of thin air.

With Cashes Secrets to Success I intend to teach you the methods that will get you started investing in real estate even if you have no money and no credit. You'll learn how to buy property with no money down... How to select flexible sellers and the right properties... How to qualify the seller and make an offer that is satisfactory for both you and the seller.... I'll show you where to go to find the most accurate and fair market values.... You'll learn how to get money back at closing and much, much more.

This course is only the beginning, a self disciplined way to succeed and the tools to get you started all I ask from you is a commitment to study the material that I give you and continually seek education, I also expect you to set aside a few hours each week to use what you have learned.

The only thing that this course lacks is the regiment of a preset schedule; a predetermined schedule makes up for a lack of self-discipline. That is why I stress the importance of making a definite commitment to set aside a time each day to study, absorb, and use what I am willing to give you as a gift from my heart.

This home study course will change your life and give you the opportunity to achieve your goals and reach your ultimate dreams. Knowledge is the only true way to success, if you give an illiterate man a million dollars he'll be broke in no time at all but on the other hand if you take a million dollars away from a knowledgeable man he'll have it all back in a very short time.

I am assuming that this endeavor will take approximately 6 months. It is my intention to relearn, refresh, and add to my knowledge so that I can not only watch you succeed but enjoy my success too.

First I want you to start by asking yourself these three questions. (1) What is my objective? (2) Is this my primary goal? (3) What am I willing to do to achieve success? When you've made a plan, take command. Remember! To make a dream a reality you have to set goals, both short term and long. To reach your goals you need a plan. Seek and you will find the way. Throughout this book I intend to help you develop that plan. A plan based on your financial situation and your unique talents and skills. Everything is possible but it's all up to you.

REMEMBER THIS; "Most failures occur as a result of bad planning or no plan at all"

YOU HAVE TO INVEST whatever it takes for the highest possible return. Whether you have 5 hours or 40 hours to spend each week you have to organize your time so that you spend it thoughtfully, creatively, and collectively. Make each and every minute that you invest in your future count.

Success is not reserved for just the rich and famous. Anyone can find success with the right motivation. There are certain conditions that can explain the differences between those who find success and those who fail. You must have the right desire and determination to succeed, without it you'll fail. Knowledge and experience also make a difference. Then there's having the courage to try. I can list many more traits that make the difference between success and failure such as determination, discipline, commitment, drive, dedication, perseverance, organization and I'm sure there's many more.

Did you ever wonder why most people never achieve their dreams and reach their ultimate goals? Some fear success and others have no self esteem. Then, in my educated opinion are the worst, the procrastinators and the completely hopeless.

As strange as it may seem we are all equal when it comes to the time we have available to us. We have 24 hours a day, whether we use it productively or waste it that's entirely up to us. I frequently hear the complaint."I just don't have enough time." This is a cop out the truth is they don't know how to manage their time.

How well do you organize your time? I want you to make a list of how you spend your time in a 24 hour period. Start with how many hours you spent sleeping, the time you spend preparing meals and eating your meals, the time you spend getting ready for work, the amount of time you spend going and coming from work, and the hours you spend working, the time you spend watching TV and playing video games, the amount of time you spend on your computer, the time you spend for RR, and finally the time you spend doing any other things that you do. Your total, more than likely, is much more than 24 hours. Your days are busy but are they organized or productive. Determine where you can cut back or even eliminate some of these things. If you reduce the amount of time you watch TV and cut back on your sleeping time you'll have more than enough time to become a successful real estate investor.

What I'm teaching you I learned from the greatest entrepreneurs in the business. Gurus like Carleton Sheets, "How to Buy Real Estate with No Money Down"... Robert Allen, "Multiple Streams of Income"... Jim Edwards, "7 Day E-Book... "Shawn Casey, "Mining for Gold" and many more..... Of course you can add "Cashes Secrets to

Success" by yours truly. How can you fail with this kind of power in your realm of knowledge?

Setting Goals
And
Planning

There is one critical ingredient needed to make your dreams a reality, first you must set goals and to make them work you have to develop a plan.

Goal setting is of vital importance for your success. You could say that goals are the keys that will open the doors to your dreams. Actually goals are nothing more than realistic dreams put into words and the plan is putting those words into action. Put your dreams in writing and then develop a time frame in which to accomplish them. Most people spend more time dreaming of success then they do planning for success.

Because I consider setting goals of primary importance I'm devoting this entire section on making goals and developing a plan. I want you to spend a great amount of time and effort establishing your goals. I'm sure that you will find as I have found that all of the rich and famous and those truly successful have set goals to get them where they are today. Setting goals is first and utmost the most important part of your journey to success and financial freedom.

There are two kinds of goals that I want you to work on. First short term goals (goals that you want to reach in a year) and second long term goals (goals that are extended five years or more).
Make a list of all the things that you want to achieve at the end of one year. Make it flexible and as realistic as possible. Don't waste your time planning for something that is out of reach or impossible.

This is an example of how I would put a short term goal in writing..........

MY GOALS FOR THE NEXT SIX MONTHS
Goal #1.
In three months I want to firmly establish myself as a seasoned real estate investor.
Plan #1.
(A) Have business cards printed stating that I am an investor and I buy and sell homes. I also have several properties that I rent. (Design your cards simple and direct. Make sure your name and phone number is in bold letters centered on the card.)
Distribute the cards to all my friends and acquaintances and everyone that I meet.

(B) Have flyers printed up with a catching design and basically the same information as my business card.

Distribute to the markets and retail stores where I shop, at the homes in the neighborhoods I farm, at gas stations and cafes. (Display them on the bulletin boards where I can.)

(C) Run ads in the local papers letting know who I am and what I do.

(D) Use the classified ads to find flexible sellers. Phone them and let them know what I do.

(E) Always dress, act and perform in a professional and seasoned manner.

Goal #2

Buy my first property in 6 months or less.

Plan #2

(A). Visit the County Courthouse and banks and look for foreclosures.

(B) Farm the neighborhoods of my choice and make lots of offers.

(C) Go through the classified section of the newspaper every day and make lots of phone calls.

This is just a sample but, as you can see, I've made a plan to accomplish each goal.

Setting long term goals are done in the same manner. Each goal must have a definite plan.

By writing your goals down and displaying them in plain view where you can read them several times each day your sub conscious mind will absorb them and consequently you'll become more accountable for them. Sharing you goals with another person can also increase your commitment.

The winners are people who experience success by doing a lot of goal setting. They use setting goals to learn new skills and gain experience. Once they've achieved a goal, they pick another. For the successful people, goal setting never stops. Goal setting is like buying real estate, after you reach the first horizon all other horizons come easier. Did you ever wonder why the rich keep getting richer and more powerful? It's because they set goals and make the right plans to achieve those goals.

It's important for you to explore and plan for what you want. The goals and dreams that you set keep the human spirit alive and hopeful. Goal setting should involve all areas of your life, including health and well being, home, leisure activities, hobbies, relationships, family, and spirituality to name a few. Manageable and realistic career and personal goals help you head in the right direction. Believe me when I say that success comes to those who keep reaching for the brass ring.

Again I can't stress enough how vitally important this session on goals is. It's short and sweet and to the point and believe it or not it will help you tremendously.

You're starting out on a brand new adventure (Real Estate Investment) so let's get you started on the right foot. Let's do some serious soul searching to figure out what it is you're willing to do to succeed. What direction are you heading in right now? Are you where you want to be in life? It's time for you to stop procrastinating and get working. Make your goals, set your plans and let's get started in the right direction.

Get a diary or a Franklin Covey planner and track your achievements as well as your appointments. If you don't know the direction you're heading in, then how do you expect to get there?

You've got to implement your plan if you want to get exactly what you want. It's time to get your rear end headed in the right direction. Don't talk the talk, get yourself motivated and walk the walk.

Don't be afraid of failing the fear of failure holds most people back. I look at failure as part of the learning process. If you fail at first pick yourself up and start all over. If you don't hold back and you put your plans into action you're going to find success.

Keep yourself focused and don't get caught up in everything going on around you. Keep your sights set clearly on your goals. Remind yourself and apply yourself to utilize the most productive and profitable use of your time, after all time is precious; it's the only thing that keeps passing us by.

The Seasoned Investor

Abraham Lincoln said; "I will prepare and someday I'll Be ready."
I want you to prepare so that when you step into the market place you'll be ready. It's important that you fill the shoes of the successful and well seasoned investor. So let's begin by talking the talk and walking the walk. Make this one of your short term goals.

Short Term Goal: Let the eye of the beholder see me as a professional and seasoned investor. The target for this goal is one month.
Plan:
(1) Get my own business cards and have flyers printed. Pass them out everywhere and to everyone.
(2) Run an ad in the local newspaper.
(3) Introduce myself as an investor and let it be known that I buy, sell, lease and rent properties.
(4) Farm neighborhoods and phone the classified ad

(5) Use the tools at my command until I learn and acquire all the tools of the trade.

(6) Post this goal and the plan so that I can review it several times a day and therefore consequently take action.

Now that you have a goal and a definite plan lets discuss the addition tools essential and at the command of the seasoned investor. First you need a work place that you can call your office, preferably an extra room in your home. Furnish your office with a desk and a file cabinet, Make room on your desk for your computer, a phone with an answering machine or service (if possible a separate line from your home phone) and a fax machine. Most all of these items can be bought quite reasonably at a church store or a discount center. Get yourself a daily planner so that you can list the important things that have to be done each day. It would also be convenient if you had a Rolex for all the phone numbers you'll need at your finger tips.

The only thing that stands between a man and what he wants from life is often merely the will to try it and the faith to believe it's possible.

As a beginner and novice you can make yourself appear as a seasoned investor in a month or less. Really to become one takes many years of training and gaining knowledge. Multiple assets are involved. The following is a list of the attributes that make the ideal seasoned real estate investor. Few ever meet this criterion.

(1) Recognizes responsibility to his or hers family, friends and community.

(2) Doesn't sacrifice his or hers spiritual life for riches and fame.

(3) Is real educated with vast knowledge about real estate.

(4) Continues learning from all sources available.

(5) Knows and uses the real estate vocabulary.

(6) Is completely aware of what's going on in the local market place.

(7) Is good at making decisions

(8) Constantly sets goals and commits them to memory.

(9) Has high moral standards and keeps involved in there issues.

(10) Is more than fair with clients and uses the win /win philosophy.

(11) Is self confident and knows how to apply his or her knowledge.

(12) Finds satisfaction in showing others the way.

Wealth Out of Thin Air

To achieve success in anything you need to start with a dream. Know your dream. Know why you are doing what you are doing. Create the fire that's needed to connect you with your dream.

Create the passion you need in your pursuit of success. Create a desire to reach your achievements. Success can be yours if you have the courage to try..May your wishes all come true and they can it's all up to you.

I'm glad you decided to broaden your knowledge and let me show you the way to a rewarding and highly profitable experience. In this section you will learn how to create wealth out of thin air. Real estate can give you a current cash income, income tax benefits, a steady growth of your assets, leverage and instant equity.

When you have successfully completed this course you'll possess the knowledge and skills that will enable you to build substantial wealth through real estate ownership using little or none of your own money.

Because real estate is absolutely unique as an investment in providing a wide variety of wealth building benefits, it is literally possible to "Create wealth out of thin air."

If you follow 100 people from the day they start working until the day they retire, this is what you'll find: One will become a millionaire...four will become financially secure...five will still be working just to survive...thirty-six will be dead....and fifty-four will be dead broke... These are facts found in Gov. Statistics. It all boils down to this. Five % will prosper and ninety-five % will not. Where do you fit in?

Most people are consciously aware that at some point in time they are not going to be able to physically continue to work.. To maintain their present life style after retirement they have to prepare for it. Unfortunately not many of the preparations that people try to make for retirement work. Many are doomed from the start..Saving your way to prosperity doesn't always work. Inflation and depressions bare there effect. Most investments are risky and can wipe you out in no time at all.

Frequently, indecision about what type of investment to make has caused people to try and save money in their own way. (A percentage of each pay check is a good example.) Savings accounts, common stocks, credit unions and many other methods of putting away for retirement are tried. Not many things work but real estate investment done with the proper knowledge is by far the best wealth builder for the future.

Here are just a few of the fundamental benefits you'll get from real estate investment.

INCOME

Many investments will produce income; a spendable or positive cash flow. For instance money that comes to the investor on a weekly, monthly or annual basis. This money can be reinvested or used to improve living standards. Money from rental income that exceeds expenses is referred to as a positive cash flow.

My last purchase of real estate was a Sandy home with a market value of $119.000. I bought this home with no money down using one of the techniques that you will learn later as we continue. Having no money down doesn't mean that the seller does not get cash. It just means that the cash doesn't have to come out of your pocket. In actuality the seller received over $10,000 at the time of closing. The property had a positive cash flow (rental income minus expenses) of $254 per month. This amounted to $3048 per year. Because the property was purchased with no money down this represents a return of infinity on my investment. Even if I had come up with the $10,000 down out of my own pocket we're looking at a return on my investment of well over 25%. Many properties will generate two, three, four and even more then this amount. Real estate offers a better potential for large cash flows than any other investment.

GROWTH

In real estate growth in value is known as appreciation. Real estate has gone up in value consistently over the years, as a matter of fact, there has seldom been a year when it has not gone up. This constant appreciation has created fortunes for many investors.

TAX BENEFITS

The tax benefits on real estate come about as a result of depreciation or cost recovery. Depreciation doesn't cost the investor one cent yet it can provide an actual tax loss to offset other income. For example if you are able to save $1200 dollars in income taxes as a result of your investing that's $100 a month income that you can use however you wish.. That's $100 in addition to the cash flow that you already receive on your property.

LEVERAGE

Leverage more than any other investment benefit is responsible for creating the greatest amount of wealth for the real estate investor. Leverage is nothing more than using other people's money to accomplish your own objectives. Therefore you can well say that leverage is the heart and soul of the course that I am teaching you.

Before we go any further I want you to write this saying down in large easy to read letters and post it where you can see it several times each day. "Within me, I have the power to achieve my greatest desires; all I have to do is unleash it. I can do whatever I tell my mind to do. I can be whatever I want to be."

PERSONAL BENEFITS

As I've already stated, real estate offers not only better benefits than any other investment but also more of them. Not all of them are obvious to the average person. For example, there are additional income advantages that come from commissions and fees, Instant equity, and mortgage amortization. Personal satisfaction can be found in the traditional programs offered along with the pride of ownership and the control you gain all contribute to your personal fulfillment

CONTROL

In real estate you control your investment. In the stock market and most other investments you don't. The success of your real estate investments rest on the decisions that you make or fail to make

If you are a stock holder in a corporation you have no part in the decision regarding a product or the pricing of that product As the owner of an apartment building or rental home you may decide to improve the property, rent your apartments on a weekly or biweekly basis rather the monthly and you can even furnish your apartments to get added income.

PRIDE

When someone purchases a new car he or she takes great pride in the ownership of the shiny new vehicle. Gradually the pride diminishes as the car ages and becomes a part of routine. However that's not true with real estate. Most investors have the same pride of ownership on the day they sell it as they do on the day it was purchased.

COMMISSIONS AND FEES

If you invest in real estate with partners there is a opportunity to earn commissions or fees. For example if you bring together three partners to invest in real estate you may take an acquisition at the time you buy the property, a management fee for managing the property, and a selling fee at the time the property is sold. (Some state laws do not allow this unless you are a licensed broker.) However if you are one of the owners and the other owners agree it's legal to charge a management fee. I'll give you more info on this when we study partnerships.

INSTANT EQUITY

During the process of this course I intend to teach you how to buy property below fair market value. The result will be instant equity which will enhance and increase your net worth. More on this as we continue..

AMORTIZATION

If you buy property using leverage (other people's money) you create a debt that is paid off by the income of the property. The payments are usually made monthly reducing the amount borrowed each month. Over a period of time more of the payment goes towards reducing (AMORTIZING) the loan with less going towards the interest and more towards the principal. This will increase your equity in the property. When you take over an older mortgage the larger portion of your payment goes towards the principal giving you a larger return from your property.

PROFITS FROM SELLING RIGHTS

Money is made in real estate when you acquire it not when you sell it. However there are things that can be done to increase the value of the property at the time of sale. One way of course is learning how to negotiate a purchase price that will safely maximize your profits.

Negotiating profits by taking property as collateral over a period of years is safe and a very attractive retirement option.

PERSPECTIVE

As you can see real estate has many benefits if bought creatively with little or no money down. YOU CAN LITERALLY CREATE WEALTH OUT OF THIN AIR.

Your ability to do this will continue indefinitely into the future.. Look back over the past 150 years, where have we been? Where are we now? Where are we going?

Real estate has gone up in value on an almost uninterrupted basis since the early 1800's. Many things have had their effect on the rate of increase but none the less it's been on a consistent movement upward.

CONCLUSIONS ABOUT THE FUTURE

Real estate will continue to increase in value in the future perhaps not at the same rate that has experienced historically. Rents will more than likely go up at a faster rate than they have in the past. It's a definite conclusion that creative financing is a necessity for future success. Therefore, giving a probability of larger and larger cash flows.

"YES YOU CAN! YOU REALLY CAN CREATE WEALTH OUT OF THIN AIR."

A traveler in ancient Greece was reputed to have asked a man by the roadside for directions to a distant point. The traveler by the roadside was the great philosopher Socrates. It is said that he pointed out and gravely told the man to just make every step go in that direction. A giant success is no more than a culmination of many smaller successes.

Someone was asked how to eat an elephant. "You do it a bite at a time was the reply. So it is with accumulating wealth out of thin air in real estate. You do it a step at a time.

The problem today is that many people want to acquire wealth by pushing buttons. There are very few, if any, legal ways that you can become a millionaire over night.

However, to become a millionaire in real estate is not that difficult if you are willing to do it a step at a time.

What you've read so far is explosive and should be reviewed many times. You have the desire to redirect and achieve that's why you're still with me, so don't wait the time will never be just right, start where you stand and use the tools that you have at your command, better tools will come later.

Keep this in mind; you quit growing when you stop learning.

I'm giving you the keys to financial freedom, all you have to do is use them and success can be yours.

Review each lesson over and over and remember," Before the reward there must be labor. You must plant before you can harvest and sow in tears before you reap in joy."

Never put off until tomorrow what you can just as easily do today. This is a well known statement asking for a firm commitment. So many times when you put things off they never get done. Be firm on this policy, in the long run it can save you time as well as money.

Dynamic Credit

Building dynamic credit can greatly expand your investment opportunities. However, you really don't need good credit to get started as a real estate investor. But, good credit will vastly expand your options and therefore your acquisition opportunities. You can create or improve your credit rating history so it is reflected in your credit reports.

I'll explain the various sources of credit available to you as a seasoned real estate investor and will explore these options. As you will soon learn if you currently have bad credit or no credit at all, you can still buy your first home or investment property. However, having good credit makes the whole process a lot easier.

Let's face it; your credit can never be too good. No matter what your situation you can always use better credit. Establishing or improving whatever credit you have is an important part of getting started. While the techniques I teach have little to do with banks or mortgage companies, if you ever do choose to use them they will almost always rely on credit reports in making their decisions to lend.

There are three major credit bureaus that act as clearing houses for collecting information concerning everyone's paying habits.. Potential lenders and businesses can contact these bureaus to find out if you are a good credit risk.

A typical report contains all kinds of personal information about you. Such as, your address, phone number, job..title and description, marital status, payment schedules, credit purchases, applications, lawsuits, bankruptcies and most all other debts. They're not supposed to collect information that is seven years or older unless you've had a bankruptcy, which will stay on your file for ten years.

Credit bureaus do not verify or make value judgments on the information they collect. Lenders decide based on their own criteria so it's up to you to make sure the information on you is correct.

Write to each major credit bureau and have them send you a copy of your credit history.

When you write to these companies you must include your address, your social security card number, your date of birth, and a picture copy of your ID.

By law these companies must show you your credit file and anyone who has checked your credit in the last 30 days.

Few people do not have at least one blemish, small or large on their credit file. Find out exactly what your credit profile is and whether any flaws that exist can be corrected. For example you may have purchased an item with your credit card and for some reason returned it and you are still getting statements showing an outstanding balance..

The Federal Fair Credit Reporting Act gives you specific rights, you can dispute any inaccuracies that you find in your files. If you inform the credit bureaus of an inaccuracy they are required to investigate the claim within 30 days. They must present your claim to the source of the error. The source must report any errors they have made. The reporting agency must then give you a written report if the results of your inquiries make a change. If the dispute is not resolved you are entitled to add a short statement with your explanation.

The Federal law requires that the credit agencies give you the names of the credit bureaus that have caused your credit to be rejected.

Computerized credit screening has replaced most credit analysts. The computer is programed to look for several positive factors; home ownership, savings accounts, job stability, and income to debt ratio. Negative factors that will show up are job hopping, to many credit cards, no history of savings and low income with excessive debt.

There are a number of things that we can do to improve the potential for a positive computer screening.
(1) Make certain that the total debt that you have, including what you are trying to borrow, does increase the debt payment ratio of your gross payment ratio to more the 25% unless you are

borrowing for a mortgage and then it should not exceed 39%..

(2) If you have unrecorded short term debt (Three to six months) do not record it, or borrow the money from a friend to pay it off in order to lower your debt ratio below 25%.

(3) List the incomes of every body that shares expenses in your household.

(4) Spousal income should be listed even though it is not required that they co-sign on the note.

(5) The purpose of the loan is important. Home improvement, medical bills, debt consolidation. Stock market or vacation or less favorable.

(6) If you are self employed list yourself as the pres. Or at least give yourself a title the reflects importance. It could have an effect on how your application is rated.

(7) If you have recently changed jobs make sure you give an explanation on a separate sheet of paper.

(8) Checking and savings accounts are positive screening factors. If possible you want to open more then one of each.

(9) If you have credit cards that you are not using, close them on a temporary basis.

(10) Finally, consider typing your application information because believe it or not this is a positive factor. (That's ten ... Don't you just love lists of ten?... I do!)

Almost everyone today has at least one credit card, if you don't have one, get one. Credit cards are an easy and very important way to establish new credit. If your present credit is so bad that you've been unable to obtain one then we may have to start you out with smaller companies and gradually build up to the larger credit card companies. You should be able to get credit cards at local stores. Sears, J. C. Penney's and R C Willey's are usually easier cards to obtain.

If all efforts fail then approach a bank to open up a charge account with a credit balance. You do this by depositing $300 to $500 dollars in an account and having them extend that much credit to you. In other words you are paying in advance for charges you will make in the future. When your account balance has been depleted the bank will more than likely issue you a credit limit without further deposits.

If you already have more than one credit card you might want to use one credit card for purchasing one type of goods and services and another card for the others.

Be sure to evaluate your credit situation and maintain only as many credit cards that are practical to you

By using common sense credit cards can become a very important asset to you in buying and maintaining real estate. For very attractive real estate investments that require down payments and fix up money, credit cards with nice credit limits are essential.

The process of building your credit no matter what method you choose is a job in itself, whatever it takes is of vital importance to you...

Here's another method to improve your credit by using banks. This time we're only going to use 4 steps.

(1) Go to two or three different banks and purchase a CD in each.

(2) Go back to each bank and ask to borrow money in the same amount you invested in the CD and offer to secure the note with your CD.

(3) Take the money that you borrow and put it in an interest bearing account. This money will be used to help pay back the banks.

(4) Make a monthly payment every week for three or four weeks and then monthly payments until the loan is paid. You now have two or three banks that you can list as credit references.
Once you have completed this technique go back to the same banks and apply for unsecured loans in the amount of your original CD and make sure they are paid off as scheduled. Repeat this method over and over again and increase your credit limit each time. It works and it doesn't take anytime at all to build a powerful credit line.

As I stated earlier, good credit is not a must when buying real estate creatively. Even though having no credit or bad credit is not a problem starting out is the time to set your sights on becoming a successful long term real estate investor and to do this you should develop a systematic program for improving your credit. Let's face it, having good credit can accelerate your time frame in achieving your financial goals.

In General
Learning is Knowledge

Here's something for you to consider. When starting out on a new journey it would be ideal if we knew all the right roads to take. If everything was mapped out for us we wouldn't get lost. It's nice to be shown the way but you won't always have someone there to do this for you. You have to learn for yourself the right way to your destination. Making mistakes starts the process of learning and the more mistakes you make the more you will learn. We can't always take a detour around the troubles and difficulties that are put in our path sometimes we have to fix the problems before we can go on.

I'd like you to take the time to review everything that I've written up to this point. You'll find many hidden messages that are meant to stimulate your thought and create positive action. You have within you the ability to do anything that you set your mind to and I have the confidence that you're going to do it. If it's going to be it's up to you and me.

Repetition and review are the best way to learn and form new habits so I want you to repeat and review over and over again.

Your success as an investor depends a whole lot on how well you let the whole world know who you are. I'll give you some of the information that you need know in order to do this and let you know where to find the rest. To be real successful you have to establish yourself as a seasoned real estate investor. Like most people you are probably starting this new adventure while working 40 t0 50 hours for somebody else trying desperately to make ends meet. Since you are starting with a minimal amount of time you should spend the time as productive as possible.

A seasoned investor has the knowledge, experience, and tools necessary to do the job. However it's possible for you to perform like a professional even without experience. The knowledge is in this course and you can easily acquire the tools to begin. Once you've made up your mind to do something don't let others discourage you and influence your decision just go ahead and do it. That's what all the successful people ahead of you have done.

Great things are performed not by strength, but by perseverance. Getting started is the hardest part of any job. If you have the courage to start then with the proper motivation you will have the courage to finish. Keep away from the people who want to belittle your ambitions, small people do that, but the really great make you feel like you to can be really great.

As you experience the trip through any one of my courses you'll become aware that I use certain phrases, thoughts and ideas over and over again. I use them to stimulate and motivate your mind. By repeatedly using sayings I hope to burn them into your subconscious mind. After all they are the thoughts and ideas of some of the greatest thinkers of all time.

The most important part of establishing yourself as a seasoned real estate investor is the knowledge that you have about creative real estate investing. As we get deeper and deeper into the course, review and review until you become comfortable with all the material presented to you. Some of my students have told me that they've gone over this course a half a dozen or more times and each time they've picked up on something that they had missed previously and many questions they had were answered as well.

It is very important to know the vocabulary of real estate investment but it will come easy once you begin as an investor. However, if you want to get a head start then I would suggest buying a glossary of real estate terms and keeping it handy at all times while taking this course. Of course as I introduce new terms and words I'll give you their meanings.

Another part of establishing yourself as a seasoned real estate investor is to make sure that you've got all the tools of your trade ready and available to you. For example an extra room in your house that can be devoted to as an office. Or at least get a desk and a file cabinet to organize and hold all your paper work. I often joke that if you want to become a paper collector the best way is to become a real estate investor. Having ample storage room so that you can organize the paperwork associated with your efforts is important.

A second phone line because the telephone is a vital tool in your investing efforts.. An answering machine or voice mail service should also be given consideration.. Later on a Fax Machine, a tax machine and a computer for e-mail communication.

In your search for a home or investment real estate, you are going to be looking for three basic categories of sellers; sellers that are flexible, sellers that may become flexible, and sellers who are inflexible but who will sell their property to you in a way that's traditional to them and a creative way to purchase with no money down for you.

It is essential that you are able to quickly locate these sellers. By establishing and advertising yourself as a seasoned real estate investor these sellers will come to you.

The following techniques are ways that you can establish a high profile and quickly find or attract flexible sellers.. If you put into practice only a few of these ideas within the next 30 days you should be able to locate a good number of flexible sellers.

First I'll make a list and then will explore each category.

(1) Business Cards.

Design a simple card that says that you buy real estate for investment purposes. Then distribute your card to everyone that you know and every place that you go.

(2) Newspaper Ads.

Again let everyone know that you buy real estate for investment and you want to make win/win deals..

(3) Classified Ads.

By the way an ad reads you'll know how to find the flexible buyers. It's easy to spot flexible sellers by the wording of their ads. For sale or lease option is definitely a flexible seller. I need to sale my house by such and such a date, make offer. Need to sale or trade by Sunday, will trade for anything that doesn't eat.

(4) Courthouses..

Get to know your courthouse and primarily these areas; The tax Assessor's Office, Mortgage and Foreclosure Office, and all other areas where you can find important information concerning real estate.

(5) Banks.

Properties owned by banks are known as REO's and sometimes REO's are made available at below market value. To get rid of these properties sometimes the bankers are willing to make real attractive deals. I even found some that are willing to lease option properties.

(6) Agents..

Dealing with brokers and licenced real estate agents sometimes can get a little messy so learn to do most things on your own. However good relationships can be very rewarding.

(7) Flyers.

Another good way to let people know that you are around and that you are a seasoned real estate investor.

(8) Investment Clubs.

A good place to discuss investing techniques and find partners in large real estate investments.

(9) Farming
(Driving through neighborhoods).

(10) Using the computer;
self explanatory but a lesson all of it's own.

All of the things listed here are common sense tools and I intend to show you how to use each and every one of them.

If you can find an investment club in your area I heartily recommend that you join and attend the meetings on a regular basis. Not only do these clubs sponsor informative guest speakers but they also have a constant flow of update real estate information. In addition they are a great source for buying or selling property. Merely letting club members know that you are in the market for certain kinds of property in certain neighborhoods is sure to elicit responses.

Locate several neighborhoods in which to concentrate your investment activities. Once you've found the right neighborhoods make it a point to drive through them frequently. Become familiar with the boundaries, schools, bus stops, shopping areas, employment centers, expressways and recreational areas.

If you drive through these areas once or twice a week you will see a lot of real estate activity. Make notes of the people moving in and moving out and of the properties that are for sale and the properties that have been sold. If you want or need a little exercise take a walk once a week in the neighborhood of your choice and meet and greet people that you see. Make yourself known and be as friendly as you can be. Talk to the people who are walking the streets or even the people who are working in their yards, become acquainted and make yourself new friends. You'll be surprised at the flexible buyers this will bring to you. I have friends in the business that do all of their business farming neighborhoods and making new friends.

Leave your business card with all the people that you meet let them know that you are willing to give them $100 for every lead that ultimately becomes a purchase.

When you start using the techniques that I've listed you are going to generate a lot of contact with sellers. Initially, 95% of your contacts are going to be made over the telephone. It is important to generate as much information as possible on the telephone without offending the seller. For now just remember to ask all your questions in a conversational way and phrase them in such a way as not to offend the seller. Be an empathetic listener. Put yourself in the sellers place, listen and agree. Believe me you'll draw a great deal of information from your conversation.

When you talk to a seller or a buyer on the telephone, someone responding to your ad or a referral from some other source try to get all the information that you can. If you are selling a piece of property the object is to match the caller's needs to the characteristics of the property. By the same token if you are buying property then your needs and desires need to be met. The following questions will help you in your fact finding efforts if your call is from a buyer.

Example; Yes, I am a private investor and own many different properties. What kind of property are you looking for? In what area would you like to live? And what is the price range you are looking for? In order to match your needs to the existing financing on my properties, I'd like to ask you what is the largest monthly payment your budget will allow? Can you afford to make a fair down payment? If so, how much? I need to get some back ground information to determine if and how much financing I can afford to give you. Where do you work? How long have you been employed there? Have you ever owned a home before? If so, how long did you own your home? Have you ever leased optioned a property? Have you ever been through a foreclosure or a bankruptcy before?

The questions can be worked into your conversation in a way that you feel comfortable and they will supply background information not only for now but for somewhere down the road.

Getting to know your way around your county courthouse can be a gold mine in disguise. This coming week I want you to visit the county courthouse, go inside, get acquainted, and explore the reference material and records that are available to you. Make this a regular visit and practice to look up information and get to know the people that work there by name. Make it a point to know the people on a personal level. They know a lot about the local market place and are most likely aware of specific properties that are for sale. Get to know them well enough so that in some point in time you can telephone them for information about properties and foreclosures. On your first trip to the county courthouse plan to spend at least 3 or 4 hours, it's an important step and a valuable investment for your future. This is actually my first assignment to you and I rate it at utmost importance.

Get to know all that you can about the tax assessor's office, the recorder's office, and the office that handles bankruptcies and foreclosures. This is vital to you and can mean thousands of dollars in savings when investing in real estate.

The rich and famous have all taken that first step and it was a gamble they were willing to take. Be optimistic as well as realistic and eventually you'll be a winner. Remember... "Beginning is winning"...

Flexible sellers are not always down and out. Sometimes even wealthy property owners are flexible. Sometimes even sellers who are not flexible can be converted by offering a higher price in return for more favorable terms. If you can create a purchase in this manner it's what is called a win/win transaction.

Keep in mind that a seller's emotions, needs, wants and desires are constantly changing. A seller who is not flexible today may become so by tomorrow. The more you meet and deal with sellers and potential sellers, the more likely it is that you will become aware of their changing situations. It is important to do everything you can to establish yourself as a high profile investor so that you can constantly meet people.

As you look at properties, you are playing the "numbers game." It is the same game that is played in every selling situation. You have to contact a certain number of people to find people who are interested. It'in s only logical that the more people that you see or who know about you the more successful you are going to be. After a while you will know where you fit in the numbers game. Let's say that for now you have to call 25 sellers to end up looking at 5 properties, make an offer on three, and end up buying one. That's it! The Numbers Game...

As I have said before, it isn't money that makes money, its knowledge. In this lesson we will find ways of developing knowledge on our local market place. It really is essential that we select the right properties in the right neighborhoods and that's where knowledge of your farming areas becomes power.

The more knowledge that you have about the market place, the less likely you are to waste time with properties that do not offer investment potential. You have only a limited time to spend looking for a house or an investment property so it's important to spend that time wisely and productively. We don't want to buy the right property in the wrong neighborhood or the wrong property in the right neighborhood. (I hope I stated that right.)

Common sense would suggest that you are probably better off dealing with lower price homes. There are far more inexpensive homes on the market then there are moderately expensive, expensive, or ultra-expensive. Common sense tells me that if you deal in the lower half of the moderately expensive homes and the upper half of the inexpensive homes that you find yourself in the right market for the majority of the buyers and sellers. By the way these properties are referred to as the bread and butter properties of the market. They are plentiful and in demand by the largest number of people.

As you look for properties in the bread and butter range you'll find them easy to identify because they are often similar in appearance and most of them need cosmetic repairs. You'll find single, two family, three and four family rental properties similar in appearances as well. The owners of these properties are frequently forced to sell because of high maintenance, interest costs, loss of jobs, death, divorce and a host of many other reasons. Because these homes exist in large numbers finding flexible sellers is not a difficult task.

Two family and four family dwellings represent good investment opportunities but the turnover rate is much higher then single family properties. The same is true in apartment buildings and other large multi- rental units.

Offsetting the turnover rate, however, is the fact that you can buy multi-units at a far lower per unit cost then single family homes. Generally the lower the cost per unit, the easier you can structure a no money down purchase with a break even or a positive cash flow.

The following game plan should enable you to develop the knowledge you need to select the neighborhoods that you want to farm. If you're goal is to retire in 10 years, by simply buying 3 homes a year you'll have 30 homes, sell 15 and use the profits to pay down the mortgages and taxes on the remaining 15. In ten years the remaining 15 houses will generate a significant income of $10,000 or more a month and you should have a net worth approaching $1 million.

I hope the picture that I'm painting is more then sufficient enough to show you the importance of quickly developing your knowledge of the market place. To do this contact all of the following individuals and organizations for information: Real estate brokers. Real estate investors, Camber of commerce, postal employees, tax assessors, utility company employees, police, delivery persons, investment clubs, title insurance companies and bankers. These contacts all have one thing in common. Directly or indirectly, their business involves real estate, and they can help. Approach all of them in the same way and ask these 5 questions in a conversational manner.

(1) What are your observations about the real estate market in this area? Do properties frequently appear on the market for sale and , if so, do they sell quickly?
(2) Do you live in this area? Do you Like it?

(3) Would you consider investing in this area ?

(4) What kind of properties would you buy?

(5) Are there areas that seem to be going up in value faster then others.

To reinforce and add to the information that you'll be receiving, do your own scouting for details.

"IT'S UP TO YOU TO DO ALL THE THINGS IT TAKES TO CHANGE YOUR LIFE AND MAKE ALL YOUR DREAMS COME TRUE."

I've started giving you a few assignments and doing these things is a must if you truly want to become successful and financially free by becoming a seasoned real estate investor. Don't just read the material that I'm giving you, I want you to apply it, use it, do it. You've already made that commitment, so follow it through and make all your dreams come true.

Get a good Day Planner and start organizing your time and make a schedule that includes everything that I'm outlining for you. I promise you success but you have to make a plan and then stick to it.
Now before I continue where I left off, here's one more thing I want you to start doing

religiously every day. I want you to make reading the real estate classified ads and making a list of the flexible sellers that you will contact by phone. If you're serious about making this real estate investing thing a part of your life then make these things part of a daily routine.

Now let's go back to scouting and farming our selected neighborhoods. You want to get a map of the neighborhoods and then go on your own personal scouting tour. Your objective is to get acquainted with the layouts of several areas where you will eventually make your investments. You should try to make your investment activities take place within a 10 to 15 mile radius of your home.. If you are a beginner then confine yourself to neighborhoods of single family and two family homes. If you are more seasoned then add larger properties to your search. You want to meet some of the people who live and work in these areas. Ask these people these few questions to help develop information quickly.

(1) I'm thinking about buying in this neighborhood. Do you live here, have you lived here a long time?

(2) Are there many renters in this neighborhood?

(3) Do you have any idea of the price of homes in this area?

(4) Do you know what people are currently paying for rent?

(5) What do you like most about this neighborhood?

(6) What do you like least?

(7) If you were to buy rental property would you buy it in this neighborhood? oftlineWhy? Why not?

(8) Do you know of any properties that are for sale or rent.

THINK OF THE EDUCATION YOU ARE GOING TO GET OVER THE NEXT 30 TO 60 DAYS IF YOU SIMPLY GO OUT AND TALK TO PEOPLE!

Any property that doesn't exist in great numbers and yet is still in demand is considered a hole in the market place. These would be properties that are easily rented because they fill the needs of the greatest number of perspective renters. Three, four, and five bedroom homes with fenced in yards, close to schools, air conditioning, central heat, fire places, and etc. are the ideal rentals where renters like to stay for long periods of time. You may never find a property that fits all of this criteria but the more of these "in demand" characteristics", the better the investment it becomes.

In addition to the physical characteristics of the property, look for properties that have favorable financing. Properties that have existing assumable FHA or V.A. financing. These things make acquiring the property much easier. Any property with seller financing or no financing will potentially give you the flexibility you need to acquire the property with no money down.

Farming for Properties

Driving through neighborhoods looking for the properties that fit your expectations is referred to as farming. You want to farm the neighborhoods of your choice once or twice every week. Look for new real estate activities such as people moving in and out of the area, new properties for sale, vacant homes, new for sale signs and properties that have been sold. Make it a point to meet the people you see, they can be a great source of information. When you meet somebody new be sure and give them your business card and it wouldn't hurt to offer them $100 for leads on any property that you ultimately buy.

Become familiar with the neighborhood boundaries; locate the shopping areas, the schools, the parks, the churches, entrances to the freeways and anything else that draws your attention.

Before you start farming let's make sure that you've selected the right neighborhoods to make investments in. You want to select two or three large neighborhoods but before you do you'll have to do your homework. You want to learn all that you can about the overall marketplace where you're going to invest. Take the time to contact the Chamber of Commerce, local investment clubs, the Apartment Association and the local court house. It would be a good idea to join an investment club and the Apartment Association. I've found that the best information comes from these associations.

Get acquainted with the layout of the areas where you'll eventually invest. You can get a map from the local bank or the Chamber of Commerce. Try to confine your investment activities within a 10 to 15 mile radius from where you live.

Starting out I'd suggest that you deal only in single family homes with 3 bedrooms and two baths or a bath and a half bath. Look for homes that have fenced in yards, garages, central air and heating, and possibly a fireplace and a finished basement. These are the kind of homes that are the easiest to rent and keep rented so they'll make a better investment.

Creative Real Estate strategies will work in any market place providing you take action and put up the effort. The first thing to focus on when farming is to seek out the motivated sellers. The properties that you eventually end up investing in are owned by the motivated sellers.

A motivated seller is a property owner whose sole aim in life is to get rid of his property.

The truth is that motivated sellers do exist and they always will. There are always a percentage of motivated sellers in any market place and here's why... Motivated sellers and the most flexible sellers are created by personal reasons not the almighty dollar. While these situations are unique to the seller they're not unusual, actually they're patterns that play over and over.

We want to concentrate on this market of highly motivated sellers. Let me give you a few of the reasons that create flexibility through motivation. First of all there's relocation, usually a job change or a transfer or some other reason Then there's relationship problems most likely a divorce, then of course financial problems from many causes, landlords sale because they're sick and tired of tenant problems. People who inherit property don't want the involvement so there are probate problems. I could list many more but I'm sure you get the drift.

Let's look at lease options or lease purchases as a strategy to solve the problems of a motivated seller and come up with a win/win solution. As a lease option investor you'll learn several different options that will solve the sellers problems. I'll discuss one that generally works in most cases.

So that you won't put your financial future at risk I'm going to give you a cash flow formula for creating wealth that will last throughout your investing career. Learn this formula and you'll learn a strategy that is guaranteed to make large sums of money in real estate investing. You can do this without ever having credit checks or using financial institutions.

Offer to take over the payments on the sellers property for the next six years, at the same time agree on a price that you can buy the property for anytime within the next six year period. This is what's called a lease purchase or option.

Once you've found the motivated seller it's time to look through your list of hungry buyers then link the two of them together. Oh, by the way, a hungry buyer is somebody who wants to own their own home but can't qualify with hard money lenders.

The strategies that we are using works better if you have hungry buyers at your finger tips and I'll let you know how this is done as we move on.

Let's assume that you've made a deal with a motivated seller but you haven't yet found a tenant buyer to complete the transaction. It's a sweet deal and you don't want to end up walking away from it, however times running out and you've got to find a buyer fast. O. K.! Here's what you do! Set up your voice mailbox with a compelling message that will make them want to leave contact information. Widely spread the word using ads, flyers, and word of mouth that you are an investor with a nice house to show but that your primary interest is to solve people's problems. Let it be known that you can find them their dream house in a nice area and that you'll structure a deal that will make them happy.

* Make sure that you check your voice mail messages several times each day and respond to them right away. Work through the numbers on the property so that you can work them in to the buyer's situation. Make sure the house is clean and tidy so that it appeals to the buyer. Before each showing make sure you arrive at the property early to make last minute preparations.

Set up showings for the property with several qualified buyers. Make sure they all fill out applications. You can charge a fee for the applications to make sure of the buyers sincerity. Screen all the applicants and select the most qualified buyer. Call and share the news with the lucky tenant buyer. Let them know that they must let you know now because you have other buyers that are ready to go. Meet with the tenant-buyer and fill out the paper work and collect your money.

Strategy #1....I used this with terrific results.

OK, I want you to follow this closely,

(1) Let's say that you offer the fair market price for the home $200,000, Make sure you lock in the price at the present market value.

(2) Agree to take over the payments of $1400, which include insurance, taxes, principle and

interest. You'll make the payments for the next six years with the option to purchase the property at any time during that period.

(3) Now if you want to sweeten the pot you offer to give the seller $2000 down. You don't have $2000, well don't worry it's not going to come out of your pocket.

(4) Tell the seller that you'll give him the $2000 as soon as you occupy or find someone to occupy the property. It's critical that this is added to the contract, it's what's called an escape clause.

(5) Now, let's say that you've found a hungry buyer who has agreed to your terms.

(6) The buyer will rent the property for three years with an option to buy.

(7) The market for the rent in this area is $1700 a month so you ask for $1800.

(8) You also agree on a purchase price of $230,000 which will be less then market value at the end of a three year period..

Market value will be $242,000 at an annual increase of 7% for appreciation.

(8) You collect a $10,000 up front option payment. Put it in the bank and write out a check to the seller for $2000 for the down payment.

Cool...That's how it works! This wasn't a no money down deal because you get to put $8000 in your pocket. WOW.

Who's going to take care of the maintenance? Again follow
closely.

(9) Tell the seller that you are willing to take care of the first $200 in maintenance for any one month which normally will take care of 98% of the maintenance.

(10) Now you go to your buyer and suggest that since he'll soon be the owner of the property that it only stands to reason that he takes care of it's upkeep but since you don't want him to get hit with any major repairs you'll set it up so that he's only responsible for the first $200 in any one given month and you'll take care of the rest.

Therefore if anything happens that costs over $200 the seller is responsible and the buyer is responsible for up to $200 so it doesn't cost you a thing.

If the hungry buyer refinances and pays off the loan at the end of three years you'll have made a profit of over $40,000 on just this one deal.

You too can profit from deals with no liability, no risk of money, no credit required, and no obligation on your part. You can do it with options. Options are a powerful way to leverage real estate and make lots of money without any financial obligations. With an option you can purchase a property at a set price for a certain amount of time. You have the option to buy but you're not obligated to buy. However if you're the seller giving the Option, you are obligated to sell the property to the buyer within a set time frame. Can you imagine the potential you have by getting Options on properties found in your neighborhood then reselling them for large profits and the only time you use the bank is to cash your check and deposit the money?

Only a motivated seller will give you an option to buy their property. They've tried almost everything and it boils down to this, they need you and they need your help. If the seller is truly motivated they'll want you to do whatever it takes to get them out of their situation so that they can move on with their lives. Options don't work for everyone. Some sellers may need other methods and that's where creativity comes into the picture. It's important to sit down with the seller and figure out the best way to handle the situation so that everybody wins. Negotiating a win/win proposition takes understanding on your part and a great deal of faith and trust on the seller's part. If you've played your part well then you are the savior and can come up with the right solution to handle this dilemma.

There are three important factors needed to make an option purchase work. First you must find the motivated seller and this is critical for by working with a motivated seller rather than an ordinary seller you'll be able to create more profits and at the same time feel good about helping the seller solve their problems. Second you want to accurately diagnose what the sellers needs are and have enough options to put together a deal that meets those needs. Third you need a new buyer to sell the property to.

Options can be risky but if you carefully screen your tenant buyers (Hungry Buyers) and link buyers to sellers before completing the deal the outcome can be very rewarding. Make sure that all your proposals are win/win/win and that everybody comes out happy in the end.

Here's another formula that might work best for you as a beginning investor. Generate cash by flipping properties to replace your current salary or income. And continue to flip properties to generate the cash you need for further investments. When you've built up a substantial reserve then look for deals that will yield a high cash flow such as apartments, office buildings, motels, hotels, condos, resorts and so on.

By taking these steps to build wealth you can avoid the pitfalls and headaches that many investors experience from owning real estate that keeps them from attaining financial freedom.

Using purchase options will give you many streams of monthly cash flow, quick cash, and financial security. As you continue buying properties your monthly cash flow will grow and grow. With each property that you add to your portfolio you'll get substantial up front money and last but not least there's property appreciation. By adding more and more properties and structuring each deal carefully and intelligently you can earn big profits from more than one deal at the same time. If you continue with this plan of action you'll find financial security in no time at all.

Purchase option investing can be structured in such a way as to eliminate risks and give you favorable benefits. First you can do away with the traditional land lord syndrome.

As you add more and more properties to your portfolio you diversify the risks by the wide spread.. The more properties that you control the more streams of income you'll have giving you that much more spendable cash. Beats tradition, doesn't it?

People are more than willing to pay a premium for easy financing just to eliminate credit checks, banks and mortgage companies. It's a fact that if you have control of the property you can instantly increase its value and set the terms, as such, to make it easier to buy. Believe me you'll attract many tenant buyers that will jump at the chance to buy your property. You can give both the hungry tenant buyer and the motivated seller an option to have what they want and make good money by doing it. The rent to own concept has been around for a long, long time.(Charging much more for a product and making terms easy so that the buyers can enjoy it before they actually have the available funds.)

Now let's say that the motivated seller wants a down payment for their property. You can do this without taking any money out of your pocket by the way you structure the deal. Here's how! When setting up the deal with the hungry tenant buyer you'll charge an option payment, usually 5%, which you'll add to the purchase price and then credit off the purchase price when the buyer consummates the buy. If the buyer decides not to consummate the deal the option fee is non refundable. As for the down payment for the motivated seller you simply subtract that from the option fee and what's left over you put in your pocket. Make sure that you have a "subject to" clause. What this means is 'subject to" your finding a qualified tenant buyer, at which time you'll pay the down payment and consummate the deal. If by chance you don't find the buyer the deal is off. Show integrity and be fair to the seller by setting a length of time for this to take place.

 I know that this question's probably in the back of your mind. What happens if the tenant buyer decides not to exercise the option to buy? Well, not to worry, you're still left in a favorable position. For example if the first buyer drops out you just get another buyer and you stand to make a lot more money. You get to keep the option fee, which was none refundable. The property has increased in value so you can get a higher sales price. Market rents have probably gone up so you can charge a higher rent. And of course, you can charge another option fee.

 So far we've learned that when a motivated seller gives a buyer an opportunity to purchase a property using an option, the price will usually be right at the top of the current market value,. However, depending on the length of the option the price could even be higher. This would compensate for a potential increase in value due to inflation.

If near the end of the option the price given the buyer is not equivalent or higher than the option price, the buyer is not obligated and can walk away from the deal. The option money received by the seller is added to the purchase price. The tax on this money is deferred until the option is either exercised or forfeited. Money received by the seller at the end of the option is treated as a capital gain.

The seller retains ownership until the option is exercised so all the tax benefits go to the seller. The seller should never have to worry about late payments because it's specified in the option that if rent payments are not made on time the option will be forfeited. This establishes the incentive for the rent to always be paid on time.

So far we've learned a little bit about lease options, however, when buying property with little or no money down there is another technique that in some cases you may want to use. This technique is called a "Subject To". .Using the subject to technique is a method where the investor gets the title (deed) to the property without assuming the mortgage. The seller keeps the mortgage in their name but signs the deed over to the investor. Up until now we've talked about making win/win propositions but with lease options and subject to deals three parties are involved in the process, the seller, the investor, and the buyer, so you always want to create a win/win/win proposition. If it isn't possible to do this then walk away from the deal. I'll give you more information on subject to deals and when to us them as we move along. For now I want to concentrate on lease options because this is where I like to do my primary investing.

Before I go on I want you to know the difference between a lease option and a lease purchase option. A lease option gives you the right to purchase or walk away from the deal anytime within a given time period. A purchase option is where you guarantee to buy the property within a given period of time. I use lease purchases when I plan to hold on to the property for a long period of time. When I put a tenant buyer in a home I always use lease options instead of lease purchase options.

WORKING WITH REAL ESTATE BROKERS.

Real estate brokers diversify as well as specialize so with such a wide spread range of abilities it's important that you find one with the ability to fit your needs. One who is knowledgeable about the types of property that you want to buy. Unfortunately as you look for the right broker you'll find that few are acquainted, or trained in creative finance and techniques used creatively to purchase property. Most do not except these techniques primarily because they depart from the traditional norm. Sometimes you have no choice but to work with a broker or salesperson like this. However, there are special techniques to help you work with this type of listing broker.

    Listing brokers are not bad people; they have the same emotions as you and I. When asked to present a creative offer with no money down they are afraid that the seller will act negatively toward them.. After all, a broker is usually working for the seller and could be accused of operating in a way contrary to the sellers best interests. When you write an offer for a property that has to go through a broker always add the words, "Buyer reserves the right to accompany broker to present offer. Brokers will act negatively to this clause but it is a simple reminder that state law, in all states, allows you to do this. Discussing this carefully with your broker beforehand should be enough to gain their cooperation.
    Always make it a point to drive your own car to the seller's home or office and arrive early, wait for the broker before you actually go to talk with the seller. Be courteous of the sellers time and always begin the conversation with "Your broker has been kind enough to allow me to explain this offer and show you how we can both benefit." Don't over do it, make it simple and clear.

Obviously I am there against the wishes of the broker but by complimenting him it starts the meeting with a positive note..

Traditionally, real estate brokers represent sellers. However, you can contract with a broker to represent you, the buyer. Rather than setting up a formal agency relationship with a broker you might simply tell the broker you would appreciate a call about any property that might fit into your guidelines. This way the broker informally becomes the buyer's broker even though the seller will be paying the commission.

Once you have found a broker to work with you, give the broker the following guidelines to identify the properties in which you might be interested.

(1) Any property owned by a flexible or highly motivated buyer.

(2) Any property the seller is willing to finance.

(3) Properties with mortgages where the outstanding balance is less then 50% of the asking price.

(4) ALL properties with assumable loans.

(5) Any property offered at 80% below market value.

If a broker can arrange for you to look at four or five properties every weekend, specially properties that fall into these guidelines, you have an excellent opportunity to buy one property a month.

I cannot over emphasize or emphasize enough the importance of finding agents and brokers who are trained in and have a positive attitude toward creative real estate finance. Try to find brokers and sales people who have previously bought investment properties themselves.

There's a new kind of broker that takes a different roll where they act as facilitators in a transaction. This posture is called the "transaction broker" and represents neither party they merely act as a go between, so to speak. Naturally if a broker is acting as a transaction broker they must disclose it in writing to all persons involved.

Motivating Thoughts

Before the reward there must be labor. You plant before you harvest. You sow in tears before you reap in joy.

Everyone who got where they are had to begin where they were. Your 0'pportunity for success is where you are right now. To attain success or to reach your goal, don't worry about having all the answers in advance. You just need to have a clear idea of your goal.

Don't procrastinate when faced with a difficult problem. Break those problems into parts, and handle one part at a time. Develop a bias toward action. You can make something happen, today.

Break your big plan for success into small steps and take the first step right away.

The highest mountain is climbed one step at a time. Take your first step today. Open your Own Doors To O'pportunity

Every situation, properly perceived, becomes an opportunity. Distant pastures always look greener than those close at hand, but opportunity lies right where you are. You must simply take advantage of them when they appear. You can start where you are at any time.

Success is all around you. It's not in your environment; it's not in luck or chance, or in the help of others. Success is in you alone.

You don't need more strength or more ability or greater opportunity. What you need is to use what you have. Learn to seize good fortune, for it is always around you. You must go to success,

it doesn't come to you.

Pit falls of a landlord

I got home from work this morning at about 0730 fed my animals, fixed myself a cup of coffee and sat down at my computer to browse the internet. First of all I checked my email to sort out all the garbage and spam. Because of my interest in real estate each day I get tons of mail from so called gurus and entrepreneurs who claim to be millionaires and out of the goodness in their hearts they're willing to show me the way to achieve my goals and become rich over night. Then there's the mail I get offering me free gifts that range from computers all the way to trips to some beautiful paradise. Finally after sorting everything out I get to open the really important stuff. Next I go to Quicken (My online banking source) where I check all my financial affairs, cleared transactions, deposits, withdrawals, and online bill payment accounts. Now, if I have time, before my daily maintenance chores as a landlord of several rental units, I like to do what I enjoy most, write.

What I've just described is routine, I do it every morning in pretty much the same order. What happens next isn't routine it's what I call the landlords Rat Race. Daily problems with my rental units and my renters that create new challenges and make life, at most, miserable.

I'm doing this in a roundabout way, but what I'm really trying to convey is that acquiring and holding on to many properties means that at some point in time the real estate investor is going to fall prey to the landlord trap. When this happens routines go out the window, habits are broken and investing stops. The investor is so busy doing maintenance and managing the properties that he already has that he doesn't have time to invest.

Let's be honest! The primary reason you are investing in real estate is because you want a better lifestyle. It doesn't make much sense if all your time is spent managing and doing maintenance on the properties you own. Because no matter how much money you're making you will still not have the freedom and quality of life that you are after.

There's a way for you to sidestep this trap and avoid all its headaches, backaches and hassles. Do you remember the strategy that I outlined for you in one of my prior lesson? The part that took care of the maintenance. It went something like this. "Mr. Seller to make this a real winning proposition for you would you like me to take care of the maintenance on a day to day bases on this property? Why don't I take care of the first $200 in any one month. That should take care of about 98% of the problems. Would that work for you?" Now you go meet with the buyer and you say, "Mr. Buyer you're coming into this property as if you are the future owner, and we expect that you'd treat the place as if it were yours. Of course this means that you are going to be responsible for the maintenance on the property. But to make it a winning proposition for you and so you'll know that you won't have any major repairs that you're responsible for, let's put a limit on it, you pay the first $200 in any one month and I'll take care of the rest.. I'll bet that wouldn't hurt your feelings. Would it?"

That's how easy it is to sidestep the landlord trap. Of course you still have the responsibility each month of collecting a check, depositing a check, and writing a check.

Working On The Phone

A very important part of real estate investing is one's ability to use the telephone effectively. As a teacher there are many things that I can convey to you but professionalism on the phone is a special art that can only be achieve by making lots and lots of phone calls. I can give you the questions that you need to get answers for but it's up to you how you work them into your telephone conversations. It's really a matter of trial and error and a whole bunch of phone calls. I suggest that you schedule a time (Right Away) to make 10 or 15 calls every day. Call the ads in the classified section of the newspaper that you feel are from flexible sellers. This is an exercise that I want you to do each day for the next two weeks. Who knows you might even find a property from a flexible buyer that you'll end up buying.. My intention however is that you learn how to feel comfortable on the phone, because in this business the telephone is one of your primary tools. If you already feel that you have a good rapport with people that you deal with on the telephone then let's make this exercise a scheduled daily routine. Remember it's still a numbers game, and whatever it takes is what you have to do. So many calls, so many contacts, so many offers and finally a deal.

Organizing the information you receive from sellers can be a nightmare if you don't have a system. Many of the properties you find, as well as many that are owned by sellers who contact you will be quickly eliminated because they don't fit your profile. If the property seems promising but the seller is totally inflexible, make a note of this on a sellers information form. Keep these notes for three to four months. If the seller is not flexible now, he or she may become flexible sometimes in the future..

If you try to contact a seller but have left only a message, make a note of it and file it under the heading, Follow up call needed. By organizing in a way that you can catalog your contacts can save you a lot of duplicate effort.

When you contact a seller or are contacted by the seller, you don't want to take up to much of the seller's time. In addition the questions you ask should be asked in a way that will not be offensive. The following questions will provide you with a prepared format for guiding the telephone conversation. Again, make sure these questions are asked in a conversational way.

This group of questions is designed to establish telephone rapport with the seller. You are asking questions which have answers that are known by the seller. Therefore they have no negative overtones. It is important to remember that establishing rapport is to be a empathetic listener.

If you receive answers that are favorable and make an appointment to see the property make sure that they are recorded on a property analysis form. (All forms can be purchased at an office supply store.)Use this form at the property to record other important information that you receive.

SPECIFIC QUESTIONS TO ASK THE SELLER

1) My name is _____. May I ask you your first name?

2) Please tell me about your home or property.

a) What is the size and sq. footage of the house.

b) What is the layout? Split plan, two story, etc...

c) What about the lot size?.
d) Does it have a garage?

e) How many rooms does it have?

f) How many full and half baths does it have?

g) What features do you consider to be special?

h) Is there any furniture or appliances included with this property?

3) What are you asking for your home? Would you mind telling me how you arrived at that price?

4) Tell me about the existing financing?

(If the seller finds this intrusive respond by telling them that as an investor you are looking for a way to purchase the property that would be a winning situation for both of us.)

5) Are you willing to assist in the financing?

Most sellers respond to this question negatively.

A. Do you need cash at the closing? How much?

B. Could the down payment be spread out over a period of time?

6) How long has the property been on the market?

7) Have you owned this property long?

8) It sounds like you have a nice home. I'm curious, why are you selling?

9) Tell me, what do you like most about your property? What do you like least?

10) Are there any renters in your neighborhood?

Do you happen to know what they're paying for rent? What do you think the rent would be on your property?

11) Would you consider leasing your property with an option to buy?

12) Quite honestly, I am a real estate investor. Let me ask you, if I were able to buy your property and pay cash and close on it in less than a week, what would be the lowest price that you would consider taking? (This plants a seed in the sellers mind that you could buy for all cash even if in reality you could not.)

13) Questions to ask the broker if one is involved.

A. Do you own any investment property yourself?

B. Have you ever owned any?

C. Does your firm manage properties?

D. If I should buy this property would you consider managing it for me? How much?

E. What is the vacancy rate in this area?

F. Do you have any properties for sale that would be a good investment for me?

G. Would you be willing to take all or part of your commission in form of a note

---

The Market Place

Whenever you see darkness, there is an extraordinary opportunity for the light to burn brighter.

Determining the value of a product or items would be easy if it was bought and sold in a perfect marketplace. Since there is no such place the stock market might be the closest. At any time of the day you can at least determine the price at which a stock is selling, thus letting you make a judgment whether you want to buy or sell.

Unfortunately real estate is not bought and sold that way. Many sellers ask what ever price they think their property is worth. Many buyers will pay a price in direct relation to the properties ability to satisfy their emotional needs. Because no two properties are alike, this makes real estate a uniquely imperfect market.

Knowledge of the real estate marketplace is critical, especially in terms of property value. The investor that knows and understands value is the one who will make a lot of money. As an investor keeping your emotional needs in check and concentrating on your financial needs is important. You cannot afford to fall in love with a property. Your sole concern should be how well the property under consideration fits your financial needs.

Money in real estate is made when you buy, not when you sell. You can't afford to accept terms today that will be unacceptable to tomorrow's buyer. Nor can you afford to buy at a price that does not allow for a reasonable profit. Don't buy what you cannot sell.

By following the guidelines that I am teaching in this course initially you will be purchasing single family homes and other small properties like two, three and four family units. You may be competing with prospective purchasers that will be evaluating these properties with an emotional bias.. This analysis tells you that the property is selling for much more then the financial analysis is worth. That's okay, move on to the next property. When you do buy property based on its true financial value you will make a profit.

Before using any other method to determine the value of real estate try using the common sense approach. While you are probably not a builder or an architect and you have not been trained to read blue prints at least you can visually try to spot potential problem areas. These will detract from the overall value of the property and will add to the cost of repairs and maintenance. Moreover if you learn to look for and identify suspected problems you may determine that professional services are needed for repairs and the best thing to do is move on to another property.

As long as you can walk, crawl and see make it a practice to systematically and completely inspect the interior and exterior of all the properties you consider for purchase.

Make a complete report evaluating the property and have the report with you each time you visit the property. The following is a check list that you should follow;

OUTSIDE
*Look for evidence of termites.
*Dry rot.
*Cracked foundations.
*Discolored roof sections.
*Sections on the roof that may need replacing.
*Missing mortar from chimney.
*Lush green grass on top of septic tank
INSIDE
*Water stains.
*Cracks in wallboards and baseboards.
*Leaks around window frames.
*windows.

*Flush toilets and turn on water facets to check for leaks and water pressure.

When you hire an appraiser to determine the value of property, the value will be appraised as of a certain date.. The price at which the appraiser arrives at is not cast in stone; it is merely the appraiser's judgment of the value of the property. Because of all the variables involved appraisers use many different ways to determine a single estimate of value. While you may not use a professional appraiser on every piece of property that you buy, you want to become familiar with the three main methods that are used..You can actually learn to use these methods without any formal training..

APPRAISAL METHOD ONE

One way to determine the value of a piece of property is to look at the price for which similar properties in the same neighborhood have recently sold. The asking price of current properties for sale is of little use. This is someone's estimate of the value, for that matter, a lets offer it for this price and see what happens approach..

While appraisers are quite scientific in the way the compare properties that have recently sold, you can do a reasonably accurate job yourself. Find one that is similar in the same neighborhood so that you can compare, "apples to apples, you might say.

You should know the approximate square footage of each property, the age, type of construction, number of bedrooms and baths, and any extra amenities the property has, such as a double garage, air conditioning, central heat, finished basement, fencing, ECT, ECT...The size of the lot can also add or detract from the price of the property.

When appraising multi-units, such as apartment buildings, and office buildings that produce rental income you should:

* compare the selling price per apartment unit by dividing the selling price by the number of apartments.

* compare the selling price by the number of square feet by dividing the selling price by the number of square feet* * * Compare the gross income multiplier, which is the selling price of the property divided by the income it generates each year. This is called the G.I.M. which I'll go into more detail as we progress.

Most of this information can be obtained through real estate brokers. T o research it yourself, public records are located in the Tax Assessors Office..

To place a value on smaller properties such as single -family and two-family homes, the market sales approach is the best and most reliable way..

APPRAISAL METHOD TWO (Reproduction cost analysis)

This method looks at the current cost of building the structure and the cost of the land.

Then subtracting the wear and tear to arrive at a value.

Costs of construction are estimated on a per square foot or cubic foot basis. Usually no attempt is made to estimate the actual cost of construction materials.

The value of the land is determined by doing a market sales analysis and learning the price of comparable lots.

Driveway and landscaping costs can be determined by the firms that specialize in these areas..

After appraising several properties you will soon have a good perspective on building costs in your area. You can then make comparisons using the info. you've gathered. However this is the least reliable way of determining value specially when it comes to older properties.

APPRAISAL METHOD THREE (Net Income Approach)

This method is used for appraising three units and up. In simple terms this approach says that the value of a property is a function of the net operating income.

The net operating income is the money that you would be able to spend if you owned the property free and clear of any mortgage or debt.

If rents increase or expenses go down the net income goes up and so does the value of the property. This is true no matter what the indicated value of the property.

If the property does not generate enough income to pay for the mortgage with a little left over for spendable cash and a positive cash flow then your option is not to buy.

I use this method when I buy investment properties that I intend to keep for an extended length of time. It works for me as a buyer but as a seller I use methods one and two.

Pre Foreclosures

First of all let me tell you what a pre foreclosure is. A pre foreclosure is the period of time during the foreclosure process between when the lender files a foreclosure lawsuit or a notice of default in the official public records and the date the property is scheduled to be sold at a public auction or trustee's sale.

The reason to consider purchasing pre foreclosures is that they supply a steady source of flexible and motivated sellers in the form of property owners that lenders have publicly declared in default. These owners face losing their properties when put on public auction via foreclosure.

Buying properties from the owners during the pre foreclosure sale period is an excellent opportunity for the investor to make large profits. Finding the sellers however, takes research and a good place to start is at the county courthouse. When a foreclosure is filed it will be assigned a case number. When you learn the case number you can obtain the file at the courthouse. The file will give you the names of the plaintiff (lender) and the defendant (borrower). You will also be able to get such information as the plaintiffs attorney, a legal description of the property, the amount of the original loan, the date of said loan, the monthly payment including the date of the last payment made and the balance owed. The records will also show any additional liens on the property.

When you've done your research and have all the information at your fingertips it's time to contact the owner, look at the property and structure a profitable deal. If you leave a card or a letter at the property address you might start it out something like this; "I invest in the properties located in this neighborhood and while checking the public records I noticed a foreclosure action against your property so I thought you might be interested in selling to resolve the problem. I try to structure deals that will remove your unfortunate situation and give you the opportunity to move on with your life. If this is the case, I've inclosed my business card, so please call me and together we can turn this into a win/win proposition."

It would be unethical for the lender to give the name or names of any individual in the rear on their payments until foreclosure action has been started. By passing out brochures flyers, and business cards to all the surrounding neighbors and leaving messages for the owner to call, usually gets results. You can approach the manager of a local loan department and ask him to let anyone who is in default or has asked for forbearance know that you can offer the help that they need. Give the manager several of your business cards to pass out to these people. Word gets around when properly spread.

Property appearance can be a dead give away to pre foreclosure prospects. People that are about to lose their homes don't care about maintenance or how their yard looks. These people are both motivated and flexible and easy to deal with.

Other ways to locate pre foreclosures, investment clubs, apartment associations, You might even find an expanded service in your market place that for a fee will give you just what you're looking for.

There are a lot of investors that work primarily on foreclosures. To eliminate the competition you want to be right up front as soon as the foreclosure suit is filed. Don't be surprised if the owner looks upon you as someone trying to take advantage of their financial situation.

If you haven't already talked to the owner greet them by saying something like this; "Hi, I'm ___ _____, I may be interested in buying your home, Do you think it would be possible for us to talk about my making an offer? Do you mind if we sit down someplace and talk about it? If the owner invites you in ask them if they'd mind showing you around the place. Before they have a chance to ask you what your offer is come right out and ask them what the lowest price is that they would consider. Make a definite appointment with the owner and ask as you are leaving if the figure they gave you is the lowest they feel they could possibly go.

Finding the owner if the property is vacant can sometimes be difficult. There are a number of ways that you can go about doing this; you already have their names from the public records so try calling directory assistance for their number. You can put a stamped envelope with a letter in their mail box and put a duplicate (without a stamp) under the front door, through a window, or inside the screen door. More than likely they'll return to pick up mail and check through the house. Another way is to get a forwarding request from the post office asking for their return address. You could call other people with the same last name. Find the attorneys name on the foreclosure suit, call him/her and ask for their name and address. Utility companies might have their billing address. If the property is occupied by a tenant renter The renter can tell you how to contact the owner. If the property is rented through a management company, the management company will know how to contact the owner.

If the absentee lives out of town then it's almost a certainty that you've found a motivated seller. Most likely the owners unaware of the run down condition of the property and because of their financial position they are unable to travel and visually inspect their property. If this is the case then the first contact with the owner should be made by a phone call then a follow up with a letter including a picture of the property to show its run down condition.

As we continue on with this lesson I want to make you completely aware of the great potential found in buying pre foreclosures at this present time. First of all lenders are making it to easy for buyers to get loans with their predatory lending practices and their lax lending policies. It all boils down to the fact that to many people are buying homes that they can't afford and so unfortunately they end up losing them by default. Sad but true, the number of homes that are foreclosed on have rapidly increased every year for the past twenty years. To many homeowners find themselves drowning in debt and subsequently live on borrowed money. Do you get the picture? Yes! It's plain to see that a smart investor can easily make millions by keeping well informed and avoiding the risks. It's not unethical nor is it something an investor should be ashamed of as a matter of fact the foreclosure investor offers much needed relief to thousands of distressed home owners each year.

As I suggested earlier, when properties are about to go into foreclosure more then likely they are run down. So when preparing to make an offer it's important to make a personal inspection to determine just how distressed the property is.

Check the outside for evidence of termites, dry rot, cracked or settling foundations, discolored roof sections and sections of the roof that may need replacing, check the chimney for loose bricks and mortar, check the grass on top of a septic tank. On the inside check for water stains, cracks in walls and baseboards, leaks around window and door frames, the windows, Check the toilets, the water faucets and the water pressure. Make an estimate of what repairs and cleanup will cost an deduct it from your final offer.

Title Companies play a very important role in your investments. The obvious routine tasks of these companies are closing transactions, handling escrows, do title searches, and providing insurance. Since it's vital that you are aware of all liens and judgments before you purchase a property the title companies service is indispensable.

.It takes knowledge and persistence to be a successful pre foreclosure investor. It doesn't take a law degree or a super high IQ but I promise you it takes a lot of hard work. T.V. gurus will tell you that if you are willing to put in five hours a week you'll reach your goals and find financial freedom. Believe me that's "Bull Crap"! Anything in this life worth having takes sacrifice and a lot of hours of hard work. As a pre foreclosure investor you first have to find the motivated and flexible sellers then there is a lot of research and property inspecting. Now you have to negotiate, buy and sell the properties and if you are knowledgeable, organized, and have that good old fashion stick-to-itiveness you'll be able to find wealth in a very competitive business. Like I said before, you don't have to be a master mind or a super mathematician but you do have to be willing to put forth the effort.

Speed and coordination are the main ingredients needed to make profits on real estate during the pre foreclosure period. Talking to the homeowner early in the pre foreclosure stage and coordinating all the information that you've gathered from the lender, the lien holders, the title company and your own analysis you can determine whether to buy quickly or move on.

To determine if there is a late payment problem just look at the property and its rundown condition. Check and see if there is a fore closure action or a published notice of default. Use any or all of the methods that I've out lined in this lesson.

Let's review what we've covered so far;

(1) Make initial contact with the homeowner. Absentee owners can be located by sending letters or with the help of the neighbors, telephone directory service or the attorney for the lender.

(2) After making contact with the owner and you have received some encouragement in terms of buying his property, analyze the property, the

neighborhood, the fair market rent value, it's resale value and the cost of repairs.

(3) Seek assistance of the title company.

(4) Talk to foreclosure lender and all lien holders to determine what discounts are available. Seek to option mortgages which can be purchased at a discount.

(5) Work out all the details with the property owner.

(6) Make sure that if you can't discount the mortgage being foreclosed that you can at least take it over with favorable terms and with the right of assumption for subsequent purchaser.

(7) Contact the title company to issue title insurance and handle closing.

(8) Record the deed and other property insurance

How to maximize your benefits by using the internet.

The world of technology is growing in leaps and bounds. We as investors can keep up with this growth by taking advantage of all the new resources made available to us by the rapid growth of technology. Advances have been swift and almost everything the consumers use is getting better and better with each passing day.

For example: Computer technology has opened the doors to a new way living. The Internet has given us access to the whole wide world. Nowhere is the power of the Internet more effective then in the real estate market. Real estate has been the fore runner to commercializing the Internet over the past 10 or 15 years. So in this lesson we're going to learn how the internet can make it easier and quicker to realize our dreams and reach financial freedom.

If you don't have computers then go out and get one. It's a small investment to make for all the huge benefits you'll get.

You can access property listings nationwide as well as in your own back yard. You'll be able to find bank owned, distressed and foreclosure properties. You'll be able to research mortgage rates, locate appraisers, insurance agents, inspectors, title companies, local investment clubs and real estate associations. You'll have round the clock access to all the information needed to buy, sell, rent or lease properties. The internet can give you access to tools that will find motivated sellers and tenant buyers. You'll be able to find out all there is to know about the market place, what market rents and home values are and that's just the beginning.

Straight from the Desk of Big Daddy Cash

Many of you are holding yourself back because you feel you don't have the money to buy real estate investments. Maybe you're not in the exact financial position you want to be in. However, you must realize that most people aren't in the most desired financial position when start out.. Many people have turned to Real Estate, because it's the ultimate leverage to earn bundles of cash without having to tie up any of their own credit. When you learn a few of the techniques, then you simply work to develop a system to repeat the process. Start slow and work your way to success a step at a time. To be successful, you must have a complete attitude change. You don't have to get all of Tony Robbins tapes you just have to change your way of thinking. Instead of thinking I don't have the money, think dam it I do, I've got more money than Carters got pills, then go out and get the job done. Money or Lack of Money is not your problem for not doing deals. As someone once told me, "If you can't do deals without money, then you can't do deals when you have money." I want you to see that lack of money is not a good reason, lack of knowledge, ambition or desire, but not lack of money. There are so many people out there that will deed their house over to you today without one red cent! As a matter of fact, some would even pay you to take over their house payments. The key is to realize that money is all around you if you've got deals in the works. If you've got a solid deal, then you can always come up with the money. But don't let lack of money be your excuse for not actively and aggressively pursuing more deals. By using Cashes Secret to Success you'll discover new ways and proven ways to generating wealth without credit checks, and the only way you'll use the bank will be to deposit more and more money. Pay close attention to Cash as he reveals his secrets on how to acquire real estate without using your own credit, without going to the bank, and without begging anyone for a loan. Believe me Cashes Secrets work. They'll work even if you have the worst credit on earth... Never worry about appreciation again because these methods are so brain dead simple anyone can do them.

Big Daddy Cash

Many of my students have broadened their knowledge with the valuable material found within the pages of this book. Unfortunately only a few know how to put that knowledge to work. Learning is one thing applying is another. I've opened the door for you that will take you in the room where all the keys to success can be found. The following is a 90 day OJT course that I've put together that will guide and direct you to your ultimate dreams. Now get off your keester and go to work.

On The Job Training ... How do I get started?

This morning one of my students called me and this is how the conversation went;

CASH: Hello, This is Cash.

JEFF: Hi Cash, This is Jeff B. I know you work nights, hope I didn't wake you up.

CASH: No, I'm just sitting here at my computer checking my email. What can I do for you?

JEFF: I have a few questions that I'd like to ask. By the way how are you feeling?

CASH: Well Jeff, I'm slightly disfigured but I'm still in the race. Was that your first question?

JEFF: Ha Ha..., No! I want you to know I think your lessons are great. I just finished your last one. It's got me all motivated and ready to go. That's one of the reasons I called.

CASH: Thanks Jeff. Have you done all the assignments I gave you?

JEFF: Yes! Now I want to get out and get some on the job training.

CASH: That's OK with me Jeff, I'm glad you're ready to take action.

JEFF: I'm ready to do whatever it takes. Problem is, I just don't know where to start.

CASH: Well Jeff, I know you're excited and anxious to start and I really want to help you, if you let me, but you'll have to do it my way. What do you say?.

JEFF: I want to make contact with a motivated seller and buy my first house right away.

CASH: That's fine Jeff, as you know some of my students have gone out and bought properties after finishing just the first three lessons.

JEFF: I know and that's what I want to do.

CASH: OK Jeff, I'm going to let you in on one of my secrets that I've yet to reveal. Please don't interrupt me and listen carefully to what I have to say. I've watched real estate investors come and go and I've noticed that the ones the buy properties before they've had a chance to get their feet wet are usually the ones that get burn out before deal number three.

JEFF: But!

CASH: Wait a minute Jeff, I asked you not to interrupt me. I'll give you a chance for a rebuttal after I'm through. What I'm telling you is not a fact, it's just an observation. I'm proud of my students that have already made purchases. However, I've already spoken to them and told them the same thing that I'm telling you. I know a lot of people that would have gone a long, long way, if they just would have slowed down and taken it a step at a time. I don't mean to burst your bubble but that's the honest to God truth. Now I'll ask you again if you still want my help and if the answer is YES we'll do it my way!!

JEFF: "WOW", now I don't know what to say.

CASH: Just give me a simple yes or no.

JEFF: Mmmmmmm......YES

CASH: OK Jeff, give me a little time to set up a game plan that will make you a success. What I want you to do today is go to your local business supply store and purchase these forms, The Sellers Information Form, The Property Analysis Form, The Property Inspection Report, The Cash Flow Form, The Property Rehabilitation Analysis, The Market Sales Form, and The Lease Option Purchase Agreement. Call me later this afternoon and we'll get you started tomorrow morning.

JEFF: Alright Cash, what time should I call?

CASH: Make it after four and before five, Bye Now

JEFF: Bye-Bye

I intend to follow this through all the way. This afternoon when Jeff calls I'll record the conversation and add it to this page.

Update; Jeff called back at 430PM

CASH: Hello, Cash speaking.

JEFF: Hi Cash, This is Jeff...How was your day?

CASH: My day was fine and how was yours?

JEFF: I spent all day studying and reviewing all of your lessons. You're right about repetition; I picked up on a lot of stuff that didn't sink in on prior reviews.

CASH: Glad to hear that Jeff. Are you ready to get started on your new career? I've got the plan of attack all ready for you.

JEFF: You bet your life! Hardly anything else has been on my mind all day.

CASH: O K, Beginning is winning so let's begin. I've set up a game plan and I'll show you the way. Pounding the beat is all up to you. Let's go to work!

I'm going to break away from the phone conversation, at least long enough to explain the step by step program that I've set up for Jeff. I've designed an on the job training program that will take a little over two months to complete. Primarily I'm doing this for Jeff; however this program will help any new real estate investor to get started on the right foot. I intend to use this mini course to help all my students get started by using the right tools of the trade.

After the first conversation when Jeff asked for my help, the idea struck me that something like this could be the incentive to motivate my students and start the ball rolling. By the way, Jeff has given me his permission to use the phone conversations in any way I see fit.

Back to the phone conversation.

JEFF: I'm listening!

CASH: The first thing I want you to do tomorrow morning is review your goals. Commit them to paper and make sure you have them with you when you leave home.

This is what I want you to do your first day on the job. Go through the yellow pages and find three title insurance companies. I want you to visit each one of these companies. Find out all that you can about their business and how they operate. Make sure you have a note book with you so you can take notes. Meet the people that work there. Jot down their names and make sure they have your name. Let them know that you're a beginning investor and that you can use all the help you can get. Title companies play a big role in your business so this is a very important first step. Do you have any questions?

JEFF: Can you suggest some title companies I can go to?

CASH: I've dealt with several different title companies but I'd rather you do the research for now. When it's time for you to pick the title company to use in your dealings and you find it hard to make a choice then I will make a few suggestions. Is that O K with you?

JEFF: Sure !

CASH: When you've accomplished this you've taken your first step. When you get home I want you to review your goals again. Ask yourself if what you did today will help you achieve your goals. Call me tomorrow evening and let me know how your day went.

JEFF: I'll give it my best shot.

CASH: Good, I'll be waiting to hear from you. Good Bye!

Jeff called me the next evening and he was bursting with enthusiasm. He had to elaborate on the vast amount of information he was able to obtain with hardly any effort. He learned about title searches and how the investigations were handled. He was able to study different types of contracts, see how escrow works, and find out about title insurance and deeds.

He said that everybody he met was willing to help him in one way or another. He said the people he met were all nice and receptive and greeted him with smiles and open arms. He said, "Cash I clicked with two of the people I met and I'm pretty sure that we'll become close friends." According to him the whole day was incredible.

The last part of his last call to me....

JEFF: Cash, all three of the places that I choose to visit were great but the one that I'll be taking most of my business to is the one where I met Sally and Jim two on first sight friends.

CASH: Jeff, I'm really glad that your first step was a success. And if you want my opinion making friends is better than making money. Good friends will always stand by you.

JEFF: You can say that again! Oh Cash, you won't believe this; I also found two neighborhoods that I want to farm. All mid range homes in nice areas, with about 500 properties in each. Sally told me what kind of properties were selling best and that both the neighborhoods I picked were in real hot marketplaces.

CASH: "WOW" You really had a successful day. I want you to spend the next two days revisiting all three of those title companies. Learn all that you can and make yourself visible. Keep reviewing your goals every morning and every evening. I also want you to reread all of the lessons I've sent you. I want you to start reading the real estate classified ads in the morning before you leave home. Just read them and see if you can pick out the flexible and motivated sellers. Highlight all the ones that you pick out and save them don't try to call them. I'll tell you why later.

Jeff ended up working the rest of the week at these three title companies.. (1) The Wasatch Title Insurance Agency in Holiday, Utah. (2) Executive Title in South Jordan, Utah. And (3) Meridian Title, in West Valley, Utah. These companies gave Jeff valuable information that will give him a head start in his new business, investing in real estate. The title company that Jeff selected to do business with was Wasatch Title the company where his special new friends work, Jim and Sally.

The second step, in week number two and three, I had Jeff visit the Salt Lake County Court House on 21 south and State St., the West Valley City Court House and the Court house in West Jordan. These three court houses are associated with the market places where Jeff picked the neighborhoods he wanted to focus on when he started farming.

I instructed Jeff to visit all the offices in these court houses that had any connection with real estate. For example, The Recorders Office, the Tax Assessors Office, and the office that handles foreclosures. I told him to introduce himself in the same manner he used when he visited the title companies and to write down all the names and telephone numbers of the people he meets that work in these offices. I want him to make himself known and make friends with as many people as he can. Jeff will add many tools to his tool box that come from these visits.

At some time at the first part of the third week I want Jeff to order business cards and flyers that he can pass out when he starts farming, this is a must. Depending on the printing company he uses this usually takes three to five days. Vista Print on the internet can get out a rush order sooner if you pay extra.

Now it's time to run ads in all the local newspapers and the free ad papers given away at markets, gas stations and restaurants. Simple ads will do fine. You want to make yourself known and at the same time find flexible buyers and sellers. If you need help with the script please call me. Usually when you place an ad if you let them know what it is for they'll help you.

Part of today's conversation with Jeff......

CASH: Well, Jeff, we've come to the end of your first month of On the Job Training. Remember to review your goals daily. Spend at least ½ hr. each morning reading the ads in the real estate classified section of the news paper, highlight the ones you feel are the most flexible but don't make any calls just yet.

JEFF: Why don't you want me to call on these ads???

CASH: Have patience my friend. This is another one of my secrets I've yet to reveal.

JEFF: Geeze Cash, why keep me in suspense?

CASH: Sorry Jeff! There's one more thing that I'd like you to do before we start on the second month. I'd like you to start meeting other investors that work in and around your area.

JEFF: How do I do this?

CASH: You can use your contacts at the title companies and the court houses. Another important source of information is the Utah Apartment Association.

JEFF: Why is it necessary for me to meet other investors?

CASH: If you know other investors that have properties they rent or lease in or around your marketplace you'll be able to tap in to critical information that will help you in making decisions before you invest.

JEFF: That makes sense. How do I get in touch with the apartment association?

CASH: That's easy Jeff. Here's their phone number (801) 506-0204 you can call them on week days between 8:30 and 5:30. I strongly recommend that you join. By using the services that they provide you can save lots of money.

JEFF: I really appreciate all the help that you're willing to give me.

CASH: Thanks, watching you succeed is achieving one of my goals. When everything is done up to this point you will have finished your first month of On the Job Training. Congratulations.

The Second Month of On the Job Training

It's very important that you keep reviewing your goals on a day to day basis. Update your daily goals as your perspective changes. Keep a diary or a log on your daily progress. Learn to take notes on the things that you want and need to remember. Good things don't just happen, you have to make them happen. Learn from your mistakes and failures don't let them discourage you. Make a strong commitment to succeed and in due process you will.

I talked to Jeff this morning and he assured me that everything that I outlined for his first month O.J.T. had been accomplished and that he was more than confidant that they were the steps that would help him achieve his long term goal. Starting out on your second month of O.J.T. (On the Job Training) you're going to farm the neighborhoods where you have chosen to make your investments. Here's a part of my first conversation with Jeff starting out the second month......

JEFF: I worked harder last month then I ever worked but you can believe me when I tell you that I enjoyed every minute.

CASH: I never promised you that it wouldn't be hard work but rests assure the rewards will be great.

JEFF: What have you got outlined for me to do starting this month?

CASH: Fill your gas tank up and make sure you have a comfortable pair of walking shoes; you're ready to start farming.

JEFF: I hoped that was coming up and I'm already prepared.

CASH: Good, I want you to drive through each of the neighborhoods that you have selected at least twice today. Observe all that you can and be sure and take notes. Each time that you drive through stop your car, get out and take a walk around a block or two. Look for people that are taking a walk, out in their front yards, or sitting on their front porch. Introduce yourself; let them know what you do, and start a casual conversation with them. I want you to have as many acquaintances as possible in each marketing area. Be sure and take notes, you want the name and addresses of your new friends.

JEFF: That doesn't sound too difficult.

CASH: It isn't, you'll probably find it fun. Don't worry about looking at any properties or making any offers today. Just get to know your market place and meet a few people.

JEFF: I'm anxious to get started.

CASH: O.K., I'll let you go now. Don't forget to read the newspaper ads and pick out the good ones, do it sometime today.

Meeting new people and making friends is a good habit to get into, It's good for business and it's good for your social life. Now that I've got Jeff out working I'll continue outlining this month's schedule.

It's very important to know your market place and getting to know the people that live there can be a good source of information. So I'm going to have Jeff continue what he's doing today for the next two days, total of three days.

When he's completed this task it's time to start looking at properties and making offers. I place a lot of importance on goals, all the rich people I know set goals all the time. So when you know what your investment goals are, knowing what kind of properties to purchase becomes critical. I advise you not to buy vacant land unless it's part of a negotiation in which case you should use it in future negotiations. My advice for the new investor is to buy three bedroom homes, there easier to flip, there easier to rent or lease for long terms, and there easier to make available on option purchase. I personally like to deal in multi unit dwellings because it allows me to gain maximum leverage with my time. Jeff has made it a point that he wants to deal primarily in option purchases and option sales. Land lording is not for him.

Finding the right property for Jeff means finding a motivated seller who is willing to be flexible, it's not really that hard there are lots of them out there. Go to my lesson about Motivated Sellers and review the whole lesson. A large part of Jeff's success investing in real estate is going to be his ability to find flexible sellers. Between 18% and 20% exist in any market place.

My conversation with Jeff as I line up his second and third coming weeks..........

JEFF: It has been a real interesting week. I've explored every nick and cranny in my market place. I've made several friends in both of my neighborhoods. I found out the some people are nice and others are not so nice. One lady told me that if I didn't get out of her sight she'd sic her dogs on me. Another called me an unmentionable and told me he never talks to strangers.

CASH: I hope your experiences didn't discourage you.

JEFF: They didn't the good out ways the bad.

CASH: I'm glad to hear that! I know I demand a lot from you but on the other hand you expect a lot out of yourself.

JEFF: I guess you're right but I'm more eager now then I've ever been. I want you to be one of the first to know. Last night I asked Sally to marry me and she said yes.

CASH: I thought there was something going on between the two of you. I'm really happy for you and let me be one of the first to congratulate you.

JEFF: Thanks! So what have you got scheduled for me. By the way Sally's going to tag along with me tomorrow. Is that all right with you?

CASH: It is, but I don't think it would make any difference. Were you able to get the names and addresses of your new friends in your market place?

JEFF: I sure did!

CASH: I want you to go buy thank you cards to send to them. Let them know how pleased you were to meet them and how talking with them was a pleasure. Tell them that you're willing to pay them $100 dollars for any leads that they give you that ultimately end up in purchasing the property. Make sure you word it right...you'll pay them only if you buy.

Now take Sally for a drive through your farming areas and stop and look at several properties. If you run into an obviously motivated seller make an offer using strategy #1 that was taught in my lesson on Motivated Sellers and Hungry Buyers. Review that lesson tonight.

Now take the rest of the week off and spend some quality time with Sally.

I've got to go now, talk to you next week.

The next few weeks of this will be spent developing your skill in your chosen trade. First we're going to start by working on the phone. As your teacher and mentor I can guide and direct you on how to buy real estate with little or none of your own money however professionalism on the phone is an art of its own and can only be learned by making lots and lots of phone calls. Review my lesson on phone calls.

O.J.T. Continues with Jeff's call for further instructions;

JEFF: Hi Cash! This is Jeff; I'm calling to see what you've got lined up for me to do this week.

CASH: I'm glad you called early because I've got a real busy day ahead of me. How was your weekend with Sally?

JEFF: We had a real great time. I like the way you put it..."Quality Time". Thanks!

CASH: I'm glad, that pleases me. Now if you don't mind we'll get right down to business. Like I said, I have a real busy day. First I want you to set up a time each day to make at least ten phone calls using the real estate classified ads that you've been saving. I want you to keep surfing the ads, highlighting the most flexible. You should spend at least ½ hour surfing the ads and however long it takes to make the phone calls. Save the new ads and use and use the ads that you've been saving.

JEFF: You said you'd reveal one of your secrets. Is this it? CASH: Yes! This is something I stumbled on quite by mistake. I've found that by using ads that are a month or two old you eliminate most of the traditional sellers thus making the motivated and flexible sellers easier to find. It works for me; I hope it works for you.

JEFF: Sounds reasonable to me, when you think about it makes a lot of sense.

CASH: Now Jeff, you're going to play the numbers game.. For every 20 calls that you make you'll probably talk with an average of 10 sellers. The rest of your calls will get you answering machines, wrong numbers, real estate agents or property managers. Out of the 10 that you talk to only two or three may qualify. What you want to do now is sort out the non-qualifying sellers quickly leaving you the potentially motivated sellers that you can spend more time with later.

JEFF: What questions should I ask the seller?

CASH: I suggest that you ask the qualifying questions first. If the seller passes then you can spend more time with them. It should only take you one or two minutes to qualify the seller. Right up front ask the seller if they would consider selling their property on a rent to own or a long term lease option if you were to guarantee that their house payments would be paid on time each month? Ask if they need cash at closing? How much? If I could come up with the cash in a week what's the lowest price you would consider? I like to buy nice houses in nice areas. Do you consider your house a nice house in a nice area?

JEFF: Wait a minute? How am I going to come up with that kind of cash?

CASH: You've just made the seller think that you have a lot of cash even though you do not. This helps to motivate the seller even that much more.

JEFF: After I've qualified the sellers what additional questions should I ask?

CASH: Here are the questions that I want you to ask the seller. Work them casually into the conversation.

(1) Give your name then ask for the sellers name......"May I please ask you for your first name."

(2) Please tell me about the property that you are selling.... The Sq. Footage....The lot size .... Does it have a garage...How many rooms and baths...Is there any furniture or appliances included?

(3) What is the asking price and how did you arrive at that price?

(4) What kind of financing do you have and who is your lender? Is the loan assumable?

(5) Are you willing to assist in the financing?

(6) Are there any renters in your area and would you happen to know what they're paying for rent? I want you to record each conversation on the Seller Information Form. File under the heading," Follow Up Call Needed."

JEFF: Wow! That sure seems like a lot to do in one day.

CASH: Oh come on! It should only take you a half day. When you get through with lunch I want you to go out and farm one of your neighborhoods, look at some properties and make another offer or two. Continue this for the rest of the week.

Jeff has decided that options are going to be his cup of tea. However, before he sets up a lease option, does a contract for deed, or buys a property that is nearing foreclosure, he'll want to have a preliminary title search done. The title search will reveal all the previous recorded documents that affect the property. Jeff has already selected the title company that he wants to use in his dealings and they can get him copies of all the documents recorded in the public records. What would be a little difficult for him, would be real easy for the title co., because they have employees that work in the courthouse every day. Of course there would be a nominal fee but for the time and work involved it will be worth it.

Now I'm going to let you in on a little more information and add to your knowledge. You've made your first steps but you still have a lot to learn.

To educate you and broaden your knowledge let me show you the way to a rewarding and highly profitable experience. You can create wealth out of thin air and I'll try to teach you how it's done. As you know, real estate gives you current cash flow income. It also gives you income tax benefits, a steady growth of your assets, leverage and instant equity.

Because real estate is absolutely unique as an investment in providing a wide variety of wealth building benefits, it is literally possible to "Create wealth out of thin air."

If you follow 100 people from the day they start working until the day they retire, this is what you'll find: One will become a millionaire...four will become financially secure...five will still be working just to survive...thirty-six will be dead....and fifty-four will be dead broke.... It all boils down to this. Five % will prosper and ninety-five % will not. Where do you fit in?

Most people are consciously aware that at some point in time they are not going to be able to physically continue to work.. So to maintain their present life style after retirement they have to prepare for it. Unfortunately not many of the preparations that people try to make for retirement work.

It's my opinion that real estate is the only sure fire method that works. Real estate has gone up in value consistently over the years, as a matter of fact, there has seldom been a year when it has not gone up. This constant appreciation has created fortunes for many investors

My last purchase of real estate was a Sandy home with a market value of $119.000. I bought this home with no money down using technique number 1... No money down doesn't mean that the seller does not get cash, It just means that the cash doesn't have to come out of your pocket. In actuality the seller received over $10,000 at the time of closing. The property had a positive cash flow (rental income minus expenses) of $254 per month. This amounted to $3048 per year. Because the property was purchased with no money down this represents a return of infinity on my investment. Even if I had come up with the $10,000 down out of my own pocket we're looking at a return on my investment of well over 25%. Many properties will generate two, three, four and even more then this amount. Real estate offers a better potential for large cash flows than any other investment.

The tax benefits on real estate come about as a result of depreciation or cost recovery. Depreciation doesn't cost the investor one red cent yet it can provide an actual tax loss to offset other income. For example if you are able to save $1200 dollars in income taxes as a result of your investing that's $100 a month income that you can use however you wish.. That's $100 in addition to the cash flow that you already receive on your property.
Leverage more than any other investment benefit is responsible for creating the greatest amount of wealth for the real estate investor. Leverage is nothing more than using other people's money to accomplish your own objectives. Therefore you can well say that leverage is the heart and soul of everything I am teaching you.

As I've already stated, real estate offers not only better benefits than any other investment but also more of them. Not all of them are obvious to the average person. For example, there are additional income advantages that come from commissions and fees, Instant equity, and mortgage amortization. Personal satisfaction can be found in the traditional programs offered along with the pride of ownership and the control you gain all contribute to your personal fulfillment.

In real estate you control your investment. In the stock market and most other investments you don't.

The decisions that you make or fail to make will determine the success of your real estate investments. If you are a stock holder in a corporation you have no part in the decision regarding a product or the pricing of that product As the owner of an apartment building or rental home you may decide to improve the property, rent your apartments on a weekly or biweekly basis rather the monthly and you can even furnish your apartments to get added income.

When you invest in real estate with partners there is a opportunity to earn commissions or fees. For example if you bring together three partners to invest in real estate you may take an acquisition at the time you buy the property, a management fee for managing the property, and a selling fee at the time the property is sold.

When you buy property below fair market value the result will be instant equity which will enhance and increase your net worth. Before we go any further I want you to write this saying down in large easy to read letters and post it where you can see it several times each day. "Within me, I have the power to achieve my greatest desires; all I have to do is unleash it. I can do whatever I tell my mind to do. I can be whatever I want to be."

When you buy property using leverage (other people's money) you create a debt that is paid off by the income of the property. The payments are usually made monthly reducing the amount borrowed each month..Over a period of time more of the payment goes towards reducing (AMORTIZING) the loan with less going towards the interest and more towards the principal. Thus increasing your equity in the property you own. When you take over an older mortgage the larger portion of your payment goes towards the principal giving you a larger return from your property.

As you develop your skill and become more seasoned you're going to find out that the real money is made when you acquire properties not when you sale them. Of course there are things that you can do to increase the property value at the time of your sale. You can structure the sale in such a way as to safely maximize your profits.

Negotiating profits by taking property as collateral over a period of years is safe and a very attractive retirement option.

Real estate will continue to increase in value in the future perhaps not at the same rate that has experienced historically. Rents will more than likely go up at a faster rate than they have in the past. All the trends point to creative financing as a necessity, with it there is a probability of larger and larger cash flows.

The problem today is that many people want to acquire wealth by pushing buttons. There are very few, if any, legal ways that you can become a millionaire over night. However, to become a millionaire in real estate is not that difficult if you are willing to do it a step at a time.

Whenever you see darkness, there is an extraordinary opportunity for the light to burn brighter. Determining the value of a product or items would be easy if it was bought and sold in a perfect marketplace. Since there is no such place the stock market might be the closest. At any time of the day you can at least determine the price at which a stock is selling, thus letting you make a judgment whether you want to buy or sell.

Unfortunately real estate is not bought and sold that way. Many sellers ask what ever price they think their property is worth. Many buyers will pay a price in direct relation to the properties ability to satisfy their emotional needs. Because no two properties are alike, this makes real estate a uniquely imperfect market.

Knowledge of the real estate marketplace is critical, especially in terms of property value. The investor that knows and understands value is the one who will make a lot of money. As an investor keeping your emotional needs in check and concentrating on your financial needs is important. You cannot afford to fall in love with a property. Your sole concern should be how well the property under consideration fits your financial needs. Money in real estate is made when you buy, not when you sell. You can't afford to accept terms today that will be unacceptable to tomorrow's buyer. Nor can you afford to buy at a price that does not allow for a reasonable profit. Don't buy what you cannot sell.

By following the guidelines that I am teaching in this course initially you will be purchasing single family homes and other small properties like two, three and four family units. You may be competing with prospective purchasers that will be evaluating these properties with an emotional bias.. This analysis tells you that the property is selling for much more then the financial analysis is worth. That's okay, move on to the next property. When you do buy property based on it's true financial value you will make a profit.

Before using any other method to determine the value of real estate try using the common sense approach. While you are probably not a builder or an architect an you have not been trained to read blue prints at least you can visually try to spot potential problem areas. These will detract from the overall value of the property and will add to the cost of repairs and maintenance. Moreover if you learn to look for and identify suspected problems you may determine that professional services are needed for repairs and the best thing to do is move on to another property.

As long as you can walk, crawl and see make it a practice to systematically and completely inspect the interior and exterior of all the properties you consider for purchase.

Make a complete report evaluating the property and have the report with you each time you visit the property. The following is a check list that you should follow;

OUTSIDE...*Look for evidence of termites...*Dry rot...*Cracked foundations...*Discolored roof sections.

*Sections on the roof that may need replacing...*Missing mortar from chimney...*Lush green grass on top of septic tank

INSIDE...*Water stains...*Cracks in wallboards and baseboards...*Leaks around window frames...*windows.

*Flush toilets and turn on water facets to check for leaks and water pressure.

When you hire an appraiser to determine the value of property, the value will be appraised as of a certain date.. The price at which the appraiser arrives at is not cast in stone, it is merely the appraisers judgment of the value of the property. Because of all the variables involved appraisers use many different ways to determine a single estimate of value. While you may not use a professional appraiser on every piece of property that you buy, you want to become familiar with the three main methods that are used..You can actually learn to use these methods without any formal training..

APPRAISAL METHOD ONE, One way to determine the value of a piece of property is to look at the price for which similar properties in the same neighborhood have recently sold. The asking price of current properties for sale is of little use. This is someone's estimate of the value, for that matter, a lets offer it for this price and see what happens approach...

While appraisers are quite scientific in the way the compare properties that have recently sold, you can do a reasonably accurate job yourself. Find one that is similar in the same neighborhood so that you can compare, "apples to apples, you might say.

You should know the approximate square footage of each property, the age, type of construction, number of bedrooms and baths, and any extra amenities the property has, such as a double garage, air conditioning, central heat, finished basement, fencing, ECT, ECT...The size of the lot can also add or detract from the price of the property.

When appraising multi-units, such as apartment buildings, and office buildings that produce rental income you should:

* compare the selling price per apartment unit by dividing the selling price by the number of apartments.* compare the selling price by the number of square feet by dividing the selling price by the number of square feet* * * Compare the gross income multiplier, which is the selling price of the property divided by the income it generates each year. This is called the G.I.M. which I'll go into more detail as we progress.

Most of this information can be obtained through real estate brokers. T o research it yourself, public records are located in the Tax Assessors Office..

To place a value on smaller properties such as single -family and two-family homes, the market sales approach is the best and most reliable way..

APPRAISAL METHOD TWO (Reproduction cost analysis)

This method looks at the current cost of building the structure and the cost of the land,hen subtracting the wear and tear to arrive at a value.

Costs of construction is estimated on a per square foot or cubic foot basis. Usually no attempt is made to estimate the actual cost of construction materials.

The value of the land is determined by doing a market sales analysis and learning the price of comparable lots.

Driveway and landscaping costs can be determined by the firms that specialize in these areas.. After appraising several properties you will soon have a good perspective on building costs in your area. You can then make comparisons using the info you've gathered. However this is the least reliable way of determining value especially when it comes to older properties.

APPRAISAL METHOD THREE (Net Income Approach)

This method is used for appraising three units and up. In simple terms this approach says that the value of a property is a function of the net operating income.

The net operating income is the money that you would be able to spend if you owned the property free and clear of any mortgage or debt.

If rents increase or expenses go down the net income goes up and so does the value of the property. This is true no matter what the indicated value of the property.

If the property does not generate enough income to pay for the mortgage with a little left over for spendable cash and a positive cash flow then your option is not to buy.

I use this method when I buy investment properties that I intend to keep for an extended length of time. It works for me as a buyer but as a seller I use methods one and two.

Have you ever played Monopoly? The great thing about Monopoly is that you can buy little green houses and trade them in for big red hotels, and use "fake" money (money that wasn't your hard earned savings). It was fun that way. There wasn't any risk involved.

Well what if you could play Monopoly in real life? You'd use leverage (other peoples money) to buy all those little green houses and create a large enough cash flow to buy bigger and better houses. Take those bigger and better houses and trade them in for a major red hotel on Park Avenue.

The amazing thing is that you can play Monopoly in real life, I can show you exactly how to buy the little "green houses" and then move up to the major "red hotels!".

Te following is a sample copy of agreement I use when the seller has said yes to all of my terms. This contract was written by me and may not be legal in your state.

_____

_____

–

OPTION LEASE/RENTAL AGREEMENT

This agreement made this ___ day of (mo.) _____ (yr.)_____, is between _____ (hereinafter called Management/Owner) and

_____ (hereinafter called Lessee). Owner leases to Resident with an option to buy, and Lesse rents from Owner with option to buy any time within a_____ year period. Residential unit is located at _____

(hereafter called premises), under the following conditions:

(1) TERM: 1. The initial term of this lease shall be _____, beginning (mo./day) _____ (yr.) _____ and ending Noon,(mo./day) _____ (yr.) _____.

(2) POSSESSION: 2. If there is a delay in delivery of possession by Management/Owner, rent shall be abated on a daily basis until possession is granted. If possession is not granted within seven (7) days after the beginning day of initial term, then Lessee may void this agreement and have full refund of deposit. Owner shall not be liable for damages for delay in possession.

(3) RENT: 3. Rent is payable monthly, in advance, at a rate of _____, per month, during the term of this agreement on the first day

of each month by direct deposit to Management/ Owners bank account

(4) DIRECT DEPOSIT: is to be paid by direct deposit on or before the first of the month.,

(5) DISCOUNT: This is a rent to own agreement and no discount will be given for early payments .

(6) LATE RENT PAYMENT AGREEMENT: This is an agreement to make payments as scheduled or lease option will be cancelled.

(7) EVICTION: If the rent called for in paragraph 3 hereof has not been paid on or before the first day of the month tenant and

possessions will be evicted from the premises.

(8) OPTION FEE DEPOSIT: Management acknowledges receipt of _____ dollars ($_____), as an option fee deposit on the first day of occupancy of the property and for Lesse's fulfillment of the conditions of this agreement. Option fee is non-refundable

(9) RENEWAL: It is the intent of both parties that this lease is for a period of _____ Should this lease be breached by the Lessee, Resident will owe rent through the last day of occupancy.

(10) SUBLET: Lessee may sublet residence or assign this lease as long as all agreements and conditions are fulfilled.

((11) MAINTENANCE: Residence agrees to pay the first $ 200 maintenance in any one given month.

(13) HOLD OVER: Lessee shall deliver possession of residence in good order and repair to Management/Owner upon termination or expiration of this agreement.

(14) RIGHT OF ACCESS: Management shall have the right of access to residence for inspection and repair or maintenance during reasonable hours. In case of emergency, Management may enter at any time to protect life and prevent damage to the property.

(15) PROPERTY LOSS: Management shall not be liable for damage to Lessee's property for any type for any reason or cause whatsoever, except where such is due to Management's gross negligence. Lessee acknowledges that he/she is aware that he/she is responsible for obtaining any desired insurance for fire, theft, liability, etc. on personal possessions, family, and guests.

(16) PETS: Animals, birds, or pets of any kind shall not be permitted inside the residential unit at any time unless the prior written

approval of Management has been obtained.

Signed by manager / owner,_____Signature of Lesse_____

One of my favorite sayings is..."If it's to be, It's up to me." When you've decided what you want whether it be wealth, independence or fame, you've made the first and most important step on your journey to success.

What I want to do for you, and I will, if you let me, is stimulate your thought process and motivate your desires. Working together will find the tools along the way. Getting started is the hardest part of any job. If you have the courage to start then with the proper motivation you will have the courage to finish.

You' find that I have repeated some of the information found in the main portion of my book. I have, because some beginning investors just use the OJT 90 day course. Don't let it bother you; repetition is a process of learning. I hope the information that I have given you makes you rich and famous or at least comfortable and secure. Good luck with your new career.

www.ingramcontent.com/pod-product-compliance
Lightning Source LLC
Chambersburg PA
CBHW022005170526
45157CB00003B/1146